PLAYING FOR CELTIC NO. 2

Champions again . . . the Celtic first team pool who clinched their fifth successive championship line-up for the camera—

top row (left to right): George Connelly, David Hay, Tommy Gemmell, John Fallon, Billy McNeill, Evan Williams, Jim Craig, John Hughes, and Tommy Callaghan.

Front row (left to right): Jimmy Johnstone, Bobby Lennox, Bobby Murdoch, Harry Hood, Willie Wallace, Bertie Auld, Lou Macari, and Jim Brogan

EDITED
BY RODGER
BAILLIE

PLAYING
FOR CELTIC
NO. 2

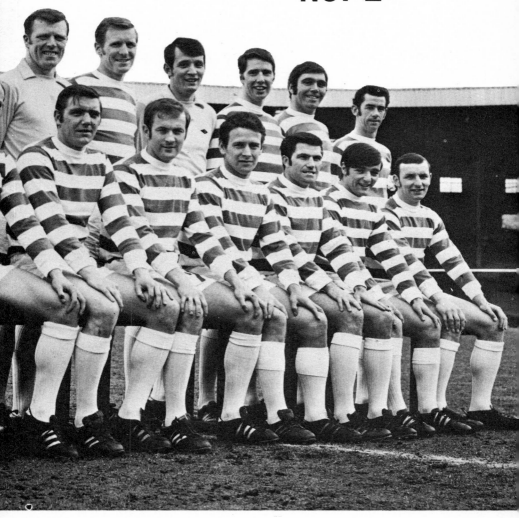

STANLEY PAUL / LONDON

STANLEY PAUL & CO LTD
178–202 Great Portland Street, London W1

AN IMPRINT OF THE HUTCHINSON GROUP

London Melbourne Sydney
Auckland Johannesburg Cape Town
and agencies throughout the world

First published 1970

*This book has been set in Baskerville, printed in Great Britain
by offset litho at Taylor Garnett Evans & Co Ltd, Watford, Herts,
and bound by William Brendon, at Tiptree, Essex*

ISBN 0 09 103340 3

Contents

Above them all . . . and yet again Billy McNeill shows how he can
outjump a defence but, sadly for Celtic, this time the ball was cleared

Victories and Defeats

THE army of fans milled about aimlessly, desperately trying to catch the unintelligible phrases pouring from the loudspeaker announcement in the hope that at last it would be their plane which would be called.

It was 7 May 1970, the day after the greatest soccer upset of the season, the defeat for Celtic by Dutch champions, Feyenoord, in the final of the European Cup.

And in Malpensa Airport, Milan, the departure point for many thousands of Celtic fans who had poured into Italy for the Final, the defeated Celtic side vainly tried to get refuge from the fans who pressed around them.

As we stood down a side corridor, manager Jock Stein, with the weariness of defeat etched on his face, said softly as if he was almost talking to himself: 'Three years ago it was wonderful to get to the European Cup Final, now we have got to win it.'

It was his reflection on the standard Celtic have set for themselves and a terse summing-up of the season's greatest achievement, reaching the final of the European Cup, and the greatest disaster, failure in the last match of the season to win it.

There is no doubt that the route to the final with the victories over Basle, Benfica, Fiorentina and Leeds United—some of them glittering masterpieces—made the hurt of the failure against Feyenoord even keener.

But success or failure in Europe is obviously set to be the soccer standard of the seventies, and it is something clubs have to live with, even if it puts an almost intolerable burden of responsibility on them.

The public have shown their insatiable demand for top-level European football. More than 20,000 Scottish fans went to Milan for the European Cup Final, many of them setting off on the trip as casually as the supporters of 20 years ago did for the farthest away fixture of that decade—a league match in Aberdeen.

And, despite the dreadful chaos of Malpensa Airport, I wonder how many will stay at home if there is another European Cup Final?

The memory of Malpensa, for me and I am sure for thousands of fans, is of an unreal nightmare.

7

The official party was more than eight hours late in taking off. They had been buffeted by the Italians, ordered out of a restaurant by police when it was supposed to be cordoned off for them, and they had been denied the haven of a V.I.P. lounge by the authorities for more than three hours.

Yet for all the trouble of delayed flights, and some of them were held up for more than 15 hours, there was very little real trouble.

Admittedly some supporters tried to rush planes when they became completely exasperated with the delays. But it was not without its typical touch of humour as fans on the tarmac shouted up to the pilots: 'Does this plane go to Glasgow?'

There were drunks around the airport, but many of them became victims because at one time the airport was selling only beer.

And fortunately the arrests for such a huge mob of fans were in the end minute. Maybe it was because the fans of Celtic and Feyenoord were friendly before, during and after the match.

Many of them swopped tammies and rosettes, some even got hold of those hideous-sounding hunting horns of the Dutch. But the handing over of colours had an ending for a few fans they could never have imagined.

Harassed airport officials were eventually reduced to waving fans on to planes merely by the scarves they wore, so some Dutch fans ended up in Glasgow and some Scottish fans in Rotterdam.

One fan got hold of a broomstick from somewhere and ran around the airport waving it like a witch, shouting: 'All this way for Glasgow.' One, blowing bagpipes led a conga-line around the airport hall.

There were enough stories to go into soccer legend, but all of it was clouded by the numbness of the failure to capture the European Cup.

Yet it was also a mark of the stature Celtic have gained in Europe, for in 1967 against Inter-Milan they had been the under-dogs, in 1970 almost every soccer expert in Europe had tipped them as favourites to beat Feyenoord.

It was the second time in a month they had failed to win a cup when they were red-hot favourites, for earlier they had lost the Scottish Cup to Aberdeen.

And it posed the question of how the team were apparently able to rise to glorious heights when many critics had written them off—for example against Leeds in the semi-final of the European Cup—but twice failed when they were expected to win.

Perhaps they will have to learn to live with the burden of being favourites in the harsh world of knock-out competitions.

The European Cup is vitally important. Especially as Scotland's international team so often falter in any competition outside the British international championship and national prestige for five successive years has really rested with Celtic.

But, while I would never downgrade its importance, there can also be a tendency to upgrade it too much.

It is after all, if a team gets to the final, only nine games. Domestic football, with its sometimes weary grind is still the passport to Europe.

That is why it is important to remember that while the European Cup eventually ended in defeat, the league championship was won in magnificent style by Celtic, 12 points ahead of their nearest rivals, Rangers.

And earlier in the season the League Cup had been captured, and a demanding challenge from the Ibrox side beaten off in the qualifying stages.

The two trophies, the League Championship and the League Cup, had in fact sat together on the Parkhead sideboard for an amazing span of five consecutive years.

The ultimate for any club is trophies in their board-room. Yet football is also a moving scene, the successful team of today may be the failures of tomorrow if they have not guarded carefully against it.

And, at a time when the team which won so much for Celtic seemed to be showing signs of stress, it must be comforting for the club, and the fans, to look at the signs for the future.

Young players were carefully brought into the first team for selected games, three of them Victor Davidson, Kenny Dalgleish and Louis Macari were taken on the North American tour.

And two of them became established members of the first-team pool. There was the success of David Hay, who either at full-back or in mid-field showed in a quietly effective way that he has all the makings of another great star for Celtic.

There was George Connelly, who had won a Cup medal in 1969 as a right-winger against Rangers, moving back to mid-field to reveal his undoubted class, especially against Leeds United.

There may be a transition period, the successes of the last few years may not be so completely overwhelming. Who knows? . . . I am a sportswriter, not an astrologist.

But whatever happens, if Celtic can continue to find youngsters of the class of player who has already made a first-team impact, then the future will be bright for them.

9

The Disaster of Milan

Bobby Murdoch turns sadly away after receiving his runners-up medal while Tommy Gemmell waits for his turn as the Dutch team Feyenoord do a lap of honour for their fans on the other side of the field

THE dreadful din of the Dutch fans' klaxon horns combined into one triumphant note of jubilation as the black-clad right arm of Italian referee Concetto Lo Bello was raised to signify the end of the fifteenth European Cup Final.

For Feyenoord, the team from the bustling seaport of Rotterdam, dismissed by almost every expert, had swept to victory against Celtic to take the European Cup.

All around the pitch of the San Siro Stadium in Milan, in moves as immaculate as their passes had been during the match, the Dutch players zoomed to one another to fall into team-mates' arms for that special brand of ecstacy that only the winning of such a major trophy can bring.

The floodlights of the giant Stadium blazed down on a scene that hardly anyone outside Holland had predicted . . . yet as the match wore on hardly anyone could see not happening.

As the delighted Feyenoord players crowded around their Austrian coach, Ernst Happel, there was another figure tugging at his arm.

It was Celtic manager Jock Stein, who had swept from his touch-line seat as soon as the final whistle had gone to dash straight to congratulate the Feyenoord coach.

I do not believe that glibly repeated phrase that no one remembers a loser in sport . . . who can recall instantly the winner of the American Masters golf tourney the year Robert De Vicenzo added up his card wrongly and lost the title?

But it is equally true that in the physically and mentally demanding world of top-class sport any professional who did not feel pain at losing should not have scaled the peaks that take him to finals in the first place.

As I studied later the close-up pictures of the Celtic players at the end of the match, they reminded me of an army who had just capitulated, the same glassy-eyed expression of disbelief that shows in the faces of prisoners-of-war.

Perhaps, at the end, they were tranquilised into almost a mild state of shock. 'Keeper Evan Williams, the man who might have been relegated into the English Third Division with Aston Villa but instead was in a European Cup Final, wept uncontrollably.

Bobby Murdoch confessed that as he walked off the pitch and saw a group of Celtic fans waving to him he felt like weeping; Bobby Lennox admitted later that he had to stop himself suddenly breaking down in a public restaurant hours after the game.

Yet it was to the credit of their manager and his team that they accepted without reservation their defeat. There has to be a loser in sport—too often the British were unhappily in that position—yet at least it is still worthy of comment when it is done at the highest level with dignity.

As the Cup was presented, the Cup that Celtic had made history by becoming the first British side to win only three years before, I looked down from the press seats high up in

Celtic skipper slides in desperately in an attempt to tackle the number one Dutch danger man, their Swedish international centre-forward Ove Kindvall

the wedding-cake tiers of the San Siro Stadium and spotted the lonely figure of Jock Stein, shoulders hunched dejectedly, slowly limping his way off the pitch to the dressing-room.

And it was outside that dressing-room half an hour later, as Europe's press pushed round him in a free-for-all scrimmage, that he admitted:

'We played badly. That sums it up, and they deserved to win. They played as a team without a weakness. Unfortunately we had too many players off form, too many bad players tonight.

'But I don't want to take anything from Feyenoord. They played well, better than us.'

Then came the question which threw a controversy around Celtic's limp performance. For a foreign journalist repeatedly interrupted to say to Stein . . . 'Yes, but why did your team play badly?'

12

As the press-men pushed around him, as the boom from a radio mike hovered only inches from his nose, the Celtic manager replied: 'I know the reasons. But they remain between myself and my players.'

It was a throw-away remark that took on almost a sinister theme as back home the soccer gossip mills of Glasgow ground out the most incredible stories about trouble between the Celtic players.

The reason for Stein's reply was simple enough. He did not feel that it was a suitable time right after the game—or indeed even later—for a public debate about his team's performance, and he protected his players when so many managers might have been tempted to shield themselves with an attack on their team.

The Celtic dressing-room was still an area of stunned silence an hour after the match. The players sat fully dressed waiting to go to the team bus, all in a similar pose, staring fixedly at the floor.

Oddly enough it was the home dressing-room used by A.C. Milan the previous season when they had only managed to draw with Celtic in a quarter-final of the European Cup.

But the contrast between defeat and victory has never been more vividly expressed than in the scenes in the Feyenoord dressing-room.

We had only been admitted for a few minutes and the champagne had just been poured into the Cup, when suddenly the door burst open and about a dozen attractive women tumbled in.

Their carefully arranged hair-styles had been disarranged in the struggle to get to the dressing-room, the mascara of some of them had run down their cheeks with the emotion of it all, but it did not matter to any of them, for they were the players' wives.

And, as each found their respective husband, towels draped round the players fell off in the scrimmage, other players jumped out of the bath to embrace their wives.

And in the shower the man who had scored the winning goal, Swedish centre-forward Ove Kindvall—his hair covered by a cap of shampoo—stood and kissed his wife.

It was a mad, mad moment of joy, the sort of scene that if a producer had put in a film he would have been accused of dreadful over-writing in the script.

They were entitled to their celebrations. The official score, flashed up on the huge electric score-board of the San Siro, read Feyenoord 2, Celtic 1 . . . but it was a travesty of a score-line.

Celtic skipper Billy McNeill,
left-back Tommy Gemmell
and goalkeeper Evan Williams
watch helpless as the header
from Feyenoord skipper
Israel gives the Dutch team
the equalising goal in the
first half in Milan (*from left
to right*)

It could easily have been 6–1, perhaps more, and it was more
a mark of the panic which enveloped the Dutch forwards in
the penalty area that it took so long to finish it off, rather than
any credit to the tattered Celtic defence.

The Celtic team was: Williams, Hay, Gemmell; Murdoch,
McNeill, Brogan; Johnstone, Lennox, Wallace, Auld, Hughes.

The first blow to the Scottish side came in only the first
minute. It was to have a stinging significance, for it was an
injury to lef-half Jim Brogan which worsened as the game pro-
gressed and eventually led to his withdrawal from the club's
close-season American tour.

Still, Celtic were making progress at the time. There were
overlapping runs down the right by David Hay, Jimmy Johnstone was probing at the Dutch defence.

And if there were doubts that the mid-field battle was swing-
ing too often Feyenoord's way they seemed to be swept away in
30 minutes when Celtic took the lead.

It came when Tommy Gemmell, yet again, hammered in a

free-kick past 'keeper Graafland, after Murdoch had flicked him a free-kick.

The omens seemed right. Gemmell had scored the first goal in Lisbon, and Stein had predicted that if Celtic got the opening score they would more easily go on to victory.

But Feyenoord had already found that this was a night when Celtic were not living up to the legend, and only two short minutes later they equalised, before the celebrations of the Parkhead fans over that goal had even died away.

There was a terrible tangle in the Celtic defence and left-back Israel popped up to head home the equaliser.

The word 'if' can be applied to sport to push forward any favourite theory, but I honestly consider that if Celtic had managed to hold that lead until half time, they would have won.

Even on level terms the Feyenoord forwards, although they could carve up the Celtic defence apparently at will, could not grab the winning goal.

Celtic centre-half Billy McNeill wins this heading joust with
Swedish centre-forward Ove Kindvall as left-back Tommy
Gemmell watches anxiously

The second half turned into a nightmare for Celtic. Their
composure was wrecked, not one of the forwards could even
get near the ball to take any pressure off a defence who were
going down quicker than the Titanic.

And everywhere on the park there seemed to be those scarlet
and white shirted Feyenoord players. They had a brilliant
general in Austrian international Franz Hasil, whose composure
spread through his side, and he was backed up by Wim Van
Hanegan, another matador who jabbed in the passes which
tortured Celtic.

George Connelly came on for Bertie Auld, and amazingly the
match moved into extra time, for truthfully it was more than
Celtic deserved.

There was one moment of hope, one single attack at the
start of extra time, when it seemed that everything would some-
how work out the way the pre-match predictions had forecast.

That was when John Hughes, at centre, made a long devastat-
ing run deep into the Feyenoord penalty area, but with only

Graafland to beat, the ball hit the diving 'keeper's legs and was eventually cleared.

The next hope was for a lifebelt of a replay. Slowly the dots on the clock on the scoreboard showed that time was running out for Feyenoord. Surely in a replay they would not outplay Celtic so much again.

Then yet again the ball sped through the Celtic defence. Centre-half Billy McNeill, harried by Kindvall, missed it with his head and shoved up his hands to touch the ball. It must have been an automatic penalty but, in the time it takes to snap your fingers, the ball broke to the Swede and he flashed it into the net.

There would be no come-back this time. The haven of full time, which Celtic had so desperately wanted, now became an enemy they wanted to avoid.

The game is over, Celtic have tasted defeat and their feelings are summed up in this picture as they line up to collect their runners-up medals. The players are *from left to right* Evan Williams, Bobby Lennox, Willie Wallace and Bobby Murdoch

Yet Feyenoord could easily have made it more, even although there were only four minutes left to play. They smashed one against the bar and should have scored another.

For me, only three players could feel they had been on form when their club needed them most: 'keeper Williams, and full-backs Hay and Gemmell.

Perhaps, too, Jimmy Johnstone who had taken dreadful punishment from a Feyenoord defence who did not believe in any ceremony about their tackling of him.

The next day was almost as bizarre in many ways. The Celtic players held a press conference, organised by their newly appointed business manager, to announce the formation of a first-team pool and that they hope to earn upwards of £40,000 a year in extra perks.

No one can object to players making sure that they are not short-changed by outside interests. Such pools are part of modern sport, but it was an unhappy time to announce its official formation so soon after such a defeat.

The ordeal for players, fans and press was not over, not by a long way. All week before the match, stories of strikes had filtered through from Italy.

There was, in actual fact, an hotel strike. It did not affect the team who were staying in Varese, an hour out of Milan. But the leading hotels in the city were not opened until the day before the game.

There were also stories that the game would not be played because of a strike of workers at the giant San Siro Stadium.

It was odd, however, that despite the prominence some papers in Scotland gave this story, at no time were the officials of either finalists told that the game was in doubt by the organisers, the European Union. And the Italian League, who were responsible for the actual arrangements, assured them it would be played . . . as indeed it was!

But the final cruel laugh from fate came at Malpensa Airport in Milan when the official party arrived to find chaos. Supporters told chilling stories of a fifteen-hour wait at the airport . . . Celtic were to suffer almost as badly.

They were eight hours late taking off, they had been chased out of a restaurant by police although it had apparently been reserved for them.

Some of the players had squatted down on the passage-ways, there was nowhere else to sit, before finally a special lounge was set aside.

Earlier the players' wives had been buffeted as they made

18

their way to the plane, and a few fans had even tried to board the plane.

It was a disgrace that the authorities had done nothing to help Celtic at the airport. It was a sad postscript to the saddest game of their season!

Swedish international centre-forward Ove Kindvall is hoisted on to a Feyenoord team-mate's shoulders as the Dutchmen celebrate their winning goal during the extra time of the European Cup Final in Milan

No More Superstitions

Do YOU dodge walking under ladders . . . look pleased when a black cat crosses your path? I suppose everyone is superstitious to some extent, but I am going to forget about it all now . . . and the match which changed my mind was the European Cup Final last season.

I hope I do not have to remind you of the score, the memory is painful enough for me.

Mind you, I would not say I was the most superstitious player in football. But I found gradually over the years I had developed a set pre-match routine—for example, I always put my pants on last—and it really became more of a habit than anything else.

Perhaps if we were having a run in some competition I would try to make sure I wore the same shirt, or the same suit, or the same tie.

But really it does not matter a button. Maybe the team that proved it all were Leeds United. They were known throughout the world of football for their pre-match routine, which was so elaborate that I sometimes wondered if they worried more about something going wrong with the preparations than the actual game.

Anyway, look what happened to them last season, despite all the supersition safeguards.

Why do so many footballers—and athletes in every sport—seem so much more superstitious than people in other walks of life?

I believe it is basically because, no matter what sport we are involved in, there is the unknown element . . . the element of chance.

Deep down I don't suppose I really believe it will affect the result because I changed my tie from one round of a competition to the next. It's merely a matter of reassurance.

Perhaps some of you saw Arsenal full-back, Bob McNab, on TV the night England lost to Brazil in the qualifying matches of the World Cup.

He had put on the same outfit which he had worn in every round of the London club's march to victory in the European Fairs' Cup . . . apart from a different tie.

Poor Bob almost seemed to have convinced himself that it was his fault England had lost that match thousands of miles away in Mexico.

There were no excuses from us for our European Cup Final defeat by Feyenoord. We were beaten that night by a better team.

I had my own personal nightmare when I literally had a

Welcome . . . to the newest member of the McNeill family, Paula Jane, from sisters Susan, Carol and Libby after the baby was born in April

hand in the Dutch side's winning goal after I had made an instinctive attempt to stop the ball breaking through to centre-forward Kindvall.

It was the second season I was involved in a goal which had helped to seal Celtic's fate in the European Cup, and my misery seemed complete when I put through my own goal in the first match of the club's North American tour against Manchester United in Toronto.

Some Canadian sportswriters almost suggested that I had a hoodoo over me for the number of goals I had been involved in, but I have never looked at it that way.

If I began to worry every time I went on the park, then I would be better retiring. After all, I have scored a few myself as well. That does not mean I do not think about how I can improve my game, but I consider that, next to the goalkeeper, I am in the most vulnerable spot in the defence.

No player is perfect, and there is going to be the odd human slip-up which no one can budget for during a game, and that will always be the way in football until the day comes when it is eleven computers against each other.

Why did we lose against Feyenoord? I wish I could give you the complete answer. The truth is we are just as puzzled about it as the many fans who travelled to Milan, and the millions who watched it on television.

Perhaps the assumption by everyone in football that we would win rubbed off on the players. But I am certain of one thing . . . it will not happen again.

Yet despite that defeat in Milan I do not accept that the season was a disaster. After all we did reach the final of the European Cup, something which for a British team to achieve only a few seasons ago would have been hailed as a miracle.

The League flag flies over Parkhead again, for the fifth successive season, and we also scooped up the League Cup.

I consider the championship achievement—and with it the right to go into Europe again—as our biggest boost.

I now have five League championship medals, yet I admit it's not so long ago that I privately began to wonder if I would ever win any medals with Celtic.

There were marvellous moments, too, in the European Cup. Who could ever forget that semi-final victory against Leeds United, the match I almost missed.

I have been pretty lucky with injuries throughout my senior career, not much more than the usual collection of knocks any player gets during a season.

Every player hopes to keep clear of injury, but that especially applies towards the end of the season if your side is in the chase for honours, and what a tightly packed fixture list we faced in the final two months of last season!

Everything was going fine for me, until the Scottish Cup Final against Aberdeen at Hampden. It happened so swiftly, so soon after the kick-off, that I hardly had time to realise I was injured.

For in only the second minute of the match I went to tackle one of the Aberdeen attack, and twisted my right ankle.

I played on, gingerly testing it every so often when the ball was at the other end of the field. Then, at the identical time in the second half, the same accident occurred again, and on the same spot.

This time I knew it could be serious. I played on, but you can imagine my feelings at the end of the game. Not only had we lost the Cup Final, but I had a huge worry about my fitness for the next Hampden date—only four days away— against Leeds in the European Cup semi-final.

The day after the Cup Final was the christening of my newest daughter, the fourth girl in the family, and I could not even get a shoe on my foot, I had to attend the service with a slipper on my right foot.

Fortunately an X-ray showed that there was no bone damage, but it was obviously going to be a race against time to get the bruising out of the injury.

I spent an anxious Monday at Parkhead. Physiotherapist Bob Rooney was wonderful. He used every method, old-fashioned remedies, plunging my foot from hot to cold baths, and even a high-pressure hose on my ankle to force away the bruising.

Then on Tuesday—the day before the match—I went down to Seamill to join the rest of the team. Frankly it was touch and go then about my fitness, and all the time the treatment continued, right up until 1 a.m. on the morning of the match.

It was doubtful almost until the kick-off, but I was anxious to play in a match of such importance. So the gamble was taken, and I am happy to say it worked out all right. But only a handful of people in that giant Hampden stadium, crammed with 135,000 people, knew how close I had been to joining them as a spectator.

That was one of my greatest moments as a Celtic player. None of us will ever forget the reception the fans gave us at the end of the match . . . maybe we should imagine we are playing English teams every match in the European Cup.

As a professional footballer I don't like having to spectate, and that goes for our four-yearly spell as the outsiders looking in at the World Cup.

I thought after the long and hectic season that Celtic had that when I returned to Scotland after the club's close-season tour I would have had enough of football.

But I was just as much bitten by the soccer television bug as anyone else, and just as despondent that Scotland had failed yet again to make the final sixteen.

I know everyone says that teams such as El Salvador, Israel or Morocco should not have been there, and the top European sides faced a much tougher qualifying section.

All that is perhaps true, but really I wonder if we can always

Number two . . . and the head that has so often helped Celtic, the head of centre-half Billy McNeill up with his attack, strikes again against Dundee United, to give him his first-ever double in one match in his senior career

blame the qualifying set-up. We have failed too often for it to be a freak result.

There are a lot of things wrong with our set-up. I still believe there is too much reliance on selectors. Whoever is the Scotland team boss must be the complete dictator, he must make up his own mind.

Selectors still dash all over the country to look at players. No doubt some of their advice is sound enough, but there's only one person who decides whether a player should be selected, and only on what he has seen, the team manager.

All great teams have been built up with one man as boss. Jock Stein with Celtic, Don Revie with Leeds, Bill Shankly at Liverpool, Harry Catterick at Everton, Bill Nicholson with

25

Spurs, Matt Busby when he was supremo with Manchester United, and—dare I say it—Sir Alf Ramsey with the England international squad.

Some officials in the not-too-distant past have not even known their own players. I shall always remember one selector saying to me after a training session for the international team . . . 'How are you feeling, John?' I looked around to see whom he was talking to, and it was a few moments before I realised he was addressing me.

I was left in no doubt he had not a clue who I was when he said to me on the day of the game . . . 'Best of luck, John.'

He could not even get my name right. I still believe, despite the statements about the freedom the present team manager, Bobby Brown, is allowed that things are not completely the way they should be.

Don't get me wrong! I am not saying I do not want to play for Scotland. That is an accusation thrown at too many players, and I just refuse to believe it is true.

I know some players have publicly said they did not want to be picked again, but I think if you analyse most of their reasons it is because of brushes with officials, or some explanation that at club level would have been sorted out much sooner.

Can there ever be any hope for us in the World Cup? Of course there is . . . Scottish teams are looked on highly in European club competitions where their record of success speaks for itself.

I believe that Bobby Brown has got the best team spirit in the present squad I have known, and that covers the last ten years.

The display in the British home international championship last season was heartening. But it must not be allowed to finish, just because we had a good result against England.

It is not for me to spell out in complete detail the troubles which afflict the Scottish team set-up. But if it ever can be sorted out I am certain we would not just be telly-viewers every four years at the World Cup.

The Spin of a Coin

THE crowd, which had surged forward like men at a bar making sure of a last drink before closing-time, suddenly split as the green-blazered figure charged through them with the force of a Rugby forward rushing for the line.

It was Celtic manager Jock Stein, pushing out of the referee's room deep in the concrete bowl of Lisbon's Stadium of

The coin that spun Celtic into the European Cup quarter-final . . . Billy McNeill holds up the Dutch 2½ guilder piece with which he won the toss against Benfica in Lisbon

Light on his way to tell his players that their captain, Billy McNeill, had won the toss against Benfica, the champions of Portugal . . . Celtic were through to the next round of the European Cup.

That was the climax to the most incredible two hours and forty minutes I have ever seen on and off a football field . . . a match which started at 9.45 p.m. on 26 November 1969 and the result was not determined until 12.25 a.m. the next morning.

Maybe that is part of the magic of the European Cup. No matter how many stamps are put in my passport as reminders of particular trips, there is always the likelihood that something different will happen, something when even the voice of the most experienced observer cannot claim he has seen it all before.

Believe me, something different happened that night!

The stark soccer outline of the story was that Celtic had gone to play Benfica in the second round of the European Cup with a handsome three-goal lead.

They had surrendered two of these goals by half time, then grimly clung to their one-goal lifeline lead to the next round until the fatal third minute of injury time when Benfica had scored again to equalise.

Thirty minutes of extra time from two teams who were almost on their knees had produced no goals.

So now the action moved off the field into a tiny, grey room off the main passageway of the unimposing entrance hall of a very imposing stadium.

It was the referee's room, and into its tight little space crowded Celtic captain, Billy McNeill, and his manager Jock Stein, Benfica skipper Mario Coluna—the coloured veteran master of football from Mozambique who had been in all of his club's four European Cup finals—the Dutch referee, Lou Van Ravens, and his two linesmen, a representative of the trophy organisers, the European Union, and a Benfica trainer.

The Portuguese club's coach, tubby little Otto Gloria, had retired to the anonymity of his team's dressing-room, the strain of the proceedings too much even for him.

Outside in the main hall, and a corridor which led off it in an L-shape design to the referee's room, players still with the sweat pouring off them on to their jerseys, officials and press-men shoved against each other in a jostling scramble to edge nearer to that tiny room.

Perhaps it was as well we did not know what was going on.

The face of despair . . . as Benfica 'keeper, Henrique, goes to pick
the ball out of the back of the net after Tommy Gemmell's
sensational opening goal

The tension outside was tremendous . . . inside it must have
been unbearable.

The fate of these two proud teams, both former winners of
Europe's most coveted trophy, was to rest on a Dutch $2\frac{1}{2}$-guilder
piece.

There were to be two calls. The first to decide which captain
would have the right to call for the actual toss to determine the
winners of the tie.

Because McNeill had been given the right to guess the spin
of the coin at the start of the game, and Coluna at the start of
extra time, it was the Celtic captain's turn again.

The coin flipped from the referee's hand up towards the
ceiling of the windowless room, as every head pushed forward
to see the result.

McNeill had called correctly, heads had been the right choice.

So now the club's European future decided simply on his choice for the second spin of the coin.

Billy decided to stick to the call of heads. I have no idea of the mathematical odds on a coin coming down twice the same way.

But as it spun upwards for the second time the plot unfolded with a twist worthy of a James Bond thriller, only this time it was so very definitely real life.

As McNeill recalled it later: 'The referee failed to catch the coin after he had spun it, and as it fell it hit him on the foot, bounced against a wall, then rolled around the floor on its edge until it went twisting down, and came up heads.'

So the silver mark of Holland's Queen Juliana blinking up at the anxious observers sealed the fate of both sides . . . for Celtic the ecstacy, for Benfica the agony.

I was one of the pack pushing outside, desperately trying to find out the result. I must admit that I thought the tie would be lost. So much had gone against Celtic that night—some of it manufactured by their own mistakes, some if it by cruel decisions—that I could not believe it would swing their way in the end.

But etched on my mind was the first sign I saw that Celtic had won—a split second before Jock Stein made his dash to his own team's dressing-room.

It was from David Hay—a reserve that night—who, standing nearest the referee's door, leapt up with his fair hair flying like a beacon in a victory salute, as the Portuguese around him seemed visibly to sag.

So we knew the result. But not the waiting fans outside, and the last act of the drama of this fantastic night had yet to come.

The crowd received a flash that Benfica had won the toss, so did millions of radio listeners all over Portugal. Alas for them! Their joy was short-lived.

Slowly, silently, they drifted away. There was no need for the guard of steel-helmeted, mounted police—grim-looking men in grey uniforms—lined up around the stadium entrance.

The crowd's feeling was matched by the deep despair I saw when I visited the Benfica dressing-room.

Some of their stars were openly weeping. Little Jimmy Johnstone came into their dressing-room to look for Eusebio, spotted captain Coluna and went to him to say: 'I am sorry it had to end this way, with one of us going out.'

And, after the initial and natural elation a more sober realisation overtook the Celtic party.

Down . . . and out! Benfica 'keeper Henrique can only clutch the post in vain as, watched by Harry Hood, Celtic's second goal from Willie Wallace speeds into the back of the net

The one that got away, for once a dash upfield, by centre-half
Billy McNeill fails to grab a goal. He beats 'keeper Henrique in the
air but the ball goes narrowly over the bar

Chairman Sir Robert Kelly, who the year before had told me
he did not approve of toss-ups or away goals counting double
to decide these ties, said they would press for a change in the rule.

Sensibly he reasoned: 'Certainly we would not have said
anything about this if we had lost the toss to Benfica. But now
that we are through, perhaps our words will carry some weight.'

Manager Stein was more blunt. He confessed later: 'I was
sick enough to pack in my job after we lost three goals.

'It's the first time since I arrived at Parkhead that the team
had lost by three clear goals. .

'It was a disgrace, carelessness caused it especially as we had
got over the worst of any away match in Europe, the first deadly
thirty minutes.

'I was relieved we had won the toss, but I was sick that we
had been forced into that position.

'However, later on I realised my first thoughts had not been
right.

'Celtic had a perfectly good goal chalked off in Glasgow, we had lost the equaliser in Lisbon well after the end of ordinary time.

'And, by at least scoring three goals in Glasgow, we had earned the right to be in the toss—even if it is an unsatisfactory way to win a game.'

So let's flashback to that game in Glasgow, with its three goals—and one disallowed—the start of the trail which was to end in that referee's room in Lisbon.

When the draw was made which paired Celtic and Benfica the Parkhead manager had commented happily, as his team were struggling slightly at the time:

'It's just the kind of challenge they need. A challenge of a team from the very top.'

Benfica chief, Otto Gloria, who had also managed Portugal when they reached the semi-finals of the 1966 World Cup, picked the league match against Ayr United at Somerset Park for his spy mission.

He sat next to Sir Robert Kelly, and with manager Stein in the row behind him in the Ayr directors' box, saw a magnificent 4–2 victory for Celtic, with two marvellous goals by Bobby Murdoch.

His prediction of the result of the European Cup match was to be proved so right . . . 'I think we will lose in Glasgow and win in Lisbon.'

Stein delayed his look at Benfica until the Sunday before the first leg in Glasgow. He flew out with worries: Celtic had stumbled to a shock 2–0 defeat from Hearts at Parkhead the day before.

But Benfica also lost, 1–0, in a local derby with their great rivals Sporting Lisbon.

And Otto Gloria summed up the feelings both managers had about their teams' defeats when he said: 'I think we lost because we were thinking more about the European Cup match.'

The Celtic manager huried back from Lisbon to take in, on the eve of the big game, at homely little Palmerston Park in Dumfries, a friendly between his reserve side and Queen of the South.

But it was to be a vital test for Willie Wallace, missing for a month from the team because of an S.F.A. suspension, to see if he could leap back into the cauldron of a European Cup tie.

He must have shown his manager enough to take the gamble, for the next night Wallace lined up at centre . . . and also in the side was left-back Tommy Gemmell, back for only his second match since he had been dropped for the League Cup Final, asked for a transfer, and been banished to the reserves.

The lure of Benifica, packed with great names of European soccer—Eusebio, Coluna, Torres—meant that 80,000, one of Celtic's biggest-ever European attendances, crammed into Parkhead.

They were not to be disappointed. Indeed if they had arrived a couple of minutes late they missed one of the most memorable goals of the season.

The scorer was Tommy Gemmell, a goal which unreeled in every watching fan the memory of his equaliser against Inter-Milan in the European Cup Final in Lisbon two years earlier.

It was set up from a free-kick by master-mind Bertie Auld, who chipped the ball neatly into the path of the onrushing full-back.

I would love to have known how fast that ball travelled as it blurred its way past Benfica's bewildered defence, and 'keeper Henrique, into the net.

Certainly the eye can be deceived. But it did seem faster than the 69.9 m.p.h. Gemmell recorded when he won the 'Sunday Mirror' Scottish Hot-shot competition, for the hardest shot in football.

And it was just too fast for some fans, never mind the Benfica defence. I heard of one man whose neighbour asked him for a cigarette light and as he turned with his lighter to shield the flame he took his eyes off the field, missed the goal, and was so incensed he promptly punched the man who had wanted the light.

Just as fascinating was the reaction of Gemmell to the goal. As he swung away around to 'The Jungle', his arm held high in a salute to the fans, it was difficult to believe here was a man who wanted to leave the club.

A controversial decision by Italian referee Concetto Lo Bello ruled out a second goal midway through the first half—which he was unable properly to explain after the game—stopped John Hughes adding to the score.

Then only minutes from half time Willie Wallace repaid his selection with the sort of goal every player dreams about . . . a goal carved out of a situation where there seems to be no danger.

Wallace cut in from the right-wing, where he had won the ball as it broke between him and a Benfica defender, and raced past another two waiting to tackle him, to clip the ball in from an almost impossible angle almost on the bye-line.

34

The great Eusebio, who had caused a few flurries in the first half, went off injured and did not reappear after the interval.

And in 69 minutes when Harry Hood got his head to a cross from Bobby Murdoch for the third goal it seemed all over . . . and, that despite some more misses, Celtic were safely through.

But manager Stein said cautiously after the game: 'It is good to be going to Lisbon three goals to the good, although you can never really get enough goals. Teams have lost such a lead before.'

Then he added exuberantly: 'But naturally I am confident that we can win through. We have not played so well all season, our fitness surprised even me.

'Winning the European Cup used to be just a dream for us.

It's No. 3 . . . as Harry Hood watches intently his header beat Benfica defence to score his side's final goal at Parkhead

Now we approach these games thinking that a final victory is always a possibility.'

Truly it had been a night of wonder. The sort of football which, when they turn it on, lifts Celtic away above even good teams, into that over-used but rarely merited accolade . . . a great side.

So it was off to Lisbon again, back to the city which will be forever linked in football history with Celtic and the European Cup.

The manager tried to set a no-nonsense attitude . . . 'It is just another job, important though it may be. It's not like the last time,' he said.

Well, it was not quite like the last time. As they trained on the neatly-manicured lawn of the luxury Palacio Hotel in Estoril—where they had warmed up only a few hours before the Final in 1967—the session had to be cut short as it poured with rain, and that had not happened the last time.

But there were an awful lot of similarities. The 1967 team, apart from Steve Chalmers, injured and not able to travel, were in the party and the day before the game against Benfica they went back to combine business and pleasure with a training session and a look at the National Stadium, where it had all happened two years before.

Yet, although they knew they were there on business, there was always the comforting thought for the Celtic players of that three-goals lead. It seemed as impregnable as France's famed Second World War defence plan, the Maginot Line, and it was to crumble about as quickly.

Before the match Celtic knew that their great rivals, Rangers, had been beaten by the Polish side, Gornik at Ibrox, and were out of the European Cup-Winners Cup.

Sadly when they heard the news it provoked cheers from some of the Celtic fans who had travelled to Lisbon. I have not the slightest doubt the same thing would have happened if Rangers had been playing abroad, and Celtic beaten at home.

Yet what a comment on the split among the fans in Scottish soccer that not even in a foreign country could they forget the twisted bitterness that passes for rivalry.

There was a tense opening half-hour for Celtic, with 80,000 fans roaring Benfica on in the Stadium of Light. The barrage was intense, John Fallon thwarted them with one great save from Eusebio, the sort of shot which had made him the telly-viewers darling in the 1966 World Cup.

However, just when they should have been easing out of

the danger period, the first breach in the Celtic defence came in 36 minutes when left-winger Simoes, out on the right, crossed and Eusebio flashed a header into the net.

Two minutes later the breach had turned into a near-flood when left-half Graca shot home a somewhat simple second.

Soon after that the game flared alarmingly into a near battle as first Auld was fouled, then Johnstone butted by right-back Silva. Incredibly the Dutch referee took no action against anyone, apart from a few fussy finger-waggings.

Celtic held out until the haven of half time, then brilliantly bossed by Billy McNeil, managed to collect their goal-shocked senses and in the second half control the game, in fact, Johnstone had a great chance to score.

Slowly, oh so slowly, the minutes ticked away right up to the 90 minutes and beyond . . . one minute, two minutes, three minutes and still no whistle came from Mr. Van Ravens.

Then, as the linesman flagged for full-time, the referee gave a foul to Benfica out on the left, no one was quite sure what was the offence.

The ball curled over, substitute Diamantino popped up to get the equaliser . . . and all hell broke loose!

The referee headed straight for the dressing-room, spectators raced on to the park, players milled about in a kaleidoscope of confusion.

Had he allowed the goal, which meant extra time, or had he blown for full time before the ball went into the net?

I dashed out of my press-box seat and sped down the tunnel to the pitch to find out what was happening on behalf of my morning paper colleagues, speaking on their phones, and unable to tell their offices back in Glasgow what was the final score.

Players stopped to ask me what was the decision, there was utter confusion, but the referee had nipped smartly to his dressing-room and when I breathlessly reached it and introduced myself on behalf of the Scottish press he told me: 'Of course, it was a goal. There will be extra time after a five-minute rest period.'

There was a nasty scene in the entrance hall when Eusebio, who had been substituted in the second-half, was involved in a near punch-up with some of the Celtic players as, nerves pushed to breaking point, everyone pushed around outside the referee's room.

Now it was extra-time. Celtic brought on Hood and Connelly for Callaghan and Auld . . . but the thirty minutes added on had all the reality of a computer contest.

37

The teams were so weary they were merely acting out the motions, it became clear that a spin of a coin was going to decide it all in the end.

So it proved, yet the drama of that incident-packed night was not confined to the pitch . . . there was just as much affecting the men who were reporting the match.

I suppose the average fan imagines that football writers sit in luxurious press boxes, picking up a phone which, when they are abroad, immediately connects them to their office on an interference-free line.

Sadly the reality is far removed from that perfect dream . . . and it did not turn out that way in Lisbon.

Around two dozen of us were packed shoulder to shoulder, into a press-box pathetically small for such a huge stadium and when the crowd in front rose from their seats, as they did frequently, it completely obscured our view.

Men are able to take TV cameras to the moon, but communication between Britain and countries such as Portugal and Spain still can prove an almost unbeatable barrier.

Hugh Taylor, of the Daily Record, struggled for the entire first half with a phone on which he could not hear a word his office in Glasgow were saying to him . . . only to return home to find out they had been able to pick up perfectly what he had been saying to them.

However the worst blow, which affected the entire press corps—and there were nine of them at the time on the phone to offices in Glasgow, Edinburgh, Dundee, Manchester and London—came just as the beginning of extra-time . . . when every phone went dead.

Apparently the phone company had only contracted the use of the extra phones at the stadium for 90 minutes, someone in the main exchange disconnected all the calls and went home.

There is no torture worse for any newspaperman anywhere than to have a story, especially of the magnitude from this match, and not be able to send it.

Back home editions were rolling with only the sketchiest information on the vital spin of the coin for it was over an hour before gradually, one by one, they were reconnected and able to spill out their stories.

I do not know who looked more shattered from the strain when everyone finally made it back to the hotel in Estoril . . . the players who had seen their lead swept away, or the newspapermen who had been left holding phones as useless to them at the vital time as a child's toy.

38

The only perverse pleasure that came out of the match was that it stilled the criticism there had been in Scotland after the first game that Benfica were a team of tired old men . . . the old men jangled their medals in that Stadium of Light.

Yet clearly Celtic should never have been in the position to depend on a toss-up, the second Lisbon story had been so different from the first.

Manager Stein put his finger neatly on the thoughts of many the next morning as he looked around the hotel, almost deserted of guests in the off-season, the swimming pool with no swimmers, and said: 'It's so different from the last time, it's just another hotel now.'

It showed that in fooball, as any other walk of life, you can't live on memories!

Congratulations! Manager Jock Stein stands on the touchline at Parkhead to acclaim his side after their victory against Benfica

Another League Cup Win

THE League Cup, dressed in its almost traditional end-of-the-Final decoration of green-and-white ribbons, was driven away from Hampden . . . back to its familiar home in the Parkhead board-room.

Yet significantly after the 1–0 victory against St. Johnstone the club had no special function that night. It was almost as if trophy-winning had become so common, so much a way of their football life, that it no longer needed to be marked by anything extraordinary.

What a change indeed from the night seven years previously when the success-starved Celtic fans had choked Glasgow's Hope Street to cheer their side, gathered for a banquet in the Central Hotel after a 3–1 defeat from Real Madrid in a charity friendly, maybe out of relief that the Spanish side, then still at the peak of their powers, had not massacred them.

I am sure there was no intention to downgrade this latest Cup victory, for in terms of soccer statistics alone it added another impressive chapter to Celtic's huge list of honours.

It was the thirteenth major honour they had won since Jock Stein returned to manage Celtic, it was their fifth successive League Cup triumph—achieved by no other side—and it was a record-breaking seventh time they had taken the trophy. You can't do much better than that!

But statistics are only the bones of any football story. The flesh and blood comes from memories—perhaps of a goal that turned a game, or a come-back which stirred the pulses. That is the real history of football.

Sometimes I feel, alas, that, by the end of a season with all its share of high drama, the League Cup, which opens the season with such a flourish, tends to have been edged out of people's memories.

A pity, for Celtic's League Cup campaign of season 1969–70 was just as hard as any of their four previous successful trophy-winning occasions.

Certainly they diced dangerously with their possession of the trophy . . . three times, at least, their grip on the Cup which had seemed as overwhelming as a lock from an all-in wrestler, became a little fragile.

Eyes front . . . all the intense concentration of an 'Old Firm' match is captured as, *left to right*, Ronnie McKinnon, 'keeper Gerry Neef, Billy McNeill, Bobby Watson and Harry Hood keep a careful eye on the ball during the League Cup match at Ibrox

For a start the draw incredibly put them, for the third successive season, in the same section as their 'Old Firm' rivals, Rangers.

Indeed, the clubs' paths seem to come together irresistibly in this competition, more often than in the Scottish Cup.

They had actually met for six successive seasons, starting with a Rangers' victory against them in the final, away back in season 1964–65, in the period the players now call B.S. . . . before Stein.

Then Celtic had won the next two finals against Rangers, before the challenge switched to the earlier qualifying stages for the next three seasons.

Many people have not been in favour of them meeting at such an early stage, and believe that the League organisers should seed the two sides to keep them separate, Celtic's deputy skipper, Bobby Murdoch, has gone on record with this view.

The other two teams in the section, Airdrie and Raith Rovers, could be grateful that at least they would make money out of the matches, but no one pretended they would be little more than making up the numbers.

The prospect of yet another early crunch between the big two meant an intensive pre-season campaign for Celtic, which actually started at the end of July because the start of the Scottish season had been brought forward to clear off all fixtures by the end of the following April to make way—what a hope it seems now—for any World Cup preparations.

So Celtic started off, on a summer's night in France, with a creditable 1–1 draw against their rivals from the previous season's European Cup, St. Etienne.

The following Saturday they travelled to Carlisle and had a jarring 1–0 defeat from the English Second Division side.

However, four days later they came back to form with a 1–1 draw in a championship of Britain battle against Leeds United at Parkhead, a marvellous display from the champions of Scotland and England.

The preparations were over, now the shooting would begin, and poor Airdrie were the first to feel the blast.

It began with a 6–1 drubbing. The Airdrie defence were so stunned at one stage that 'keeper Roddy McKenzie turned to a photographer behind the goal and help up his hand, showing first four, then five fingers. The photographer, thinking he meant how long until half time, shouted back: 'Five minutes', and was shaken by the 'keeper's reply: 'No, I didn't mean that. How many have they scored?'

42

So the stage was set for Ibrox, and the first 'Old Firm' clash of the season. Rangers' manager Davie White has said at his team's press day, before the season began:

'The best thing that could happen to our morale would be to edge Celtic out and win the League Cup. That would solve a great many of our problems. It would be a real blow to us if we were to go out.'

It was the two teams' first confrontation since the crushing Celtic had inflicted on Rangers in the previous Scottish Cup Final, and it had added spice with the appearance of Jim Baxter, back once again in a Rangers jersey.

The first success went to Celtic, when in only nine minutes Harry Hood raced on to pass down the right from John Clark, and neatly tricked the Rangers defence to score.

But Celtic had a blow in 17 minutes when Bobby Murdoch was taken off injured with a thigh injury—in fact, he was driven home at half time.

Maybe that upset their rhythm, but they should have added to their score before half time, and Celtic were to pay expensively for their failure to take their chances later in the game.

For, capsuled into two minutes in the opening spell in the second half, the game swung completely Rangers' way.

The first shock was the equaliser in 48 minutes, when a cross from right-back Kai Johansen was put into goal by Orjan Persson, left dangerously unguarded.

The second shock was only a minute later. And if the defence were still trying to sort out who was to blame for the first goal they had even more to talk about at the second, for it was certainly preventable.

A needlessly conceded free-kick gave Rangers possession on their left just outside the penalty box. Baxter took it, and as he went to kick it he saw John Greig on the right signal for it. So did everyone else in the ground, but, sadly for them, not a Celtic defender.

Greig headed it into the centre of the penalty box, and Willie Johnston scored to make it 2–1 for Rangers, the eventual result.

This was the game that got away, and Celtic's first defeat in a League Cup tie since they had lost to Dundee in 1965.

Seventy-one thousand fans had watched the match, but there was actually more trouble on the park than arrests off it, for three players had been booked: Celtic's Tommy Gemmell and Bertie Auld, and Jim Baxter of Rangers.

Rangers were ahead in the race for the qualifying spot, and with a week's breathing space before the second meeting, both sides won comfortably the following Saturday; Celtic crushed Raith Rovers 5–0 at Parkhead, Rangers won 3–0 against Airdrie at Broomfield.

Rangers, two points ahead in the section, only needed a draw at Parkhead to make virtually sure of that quarter-final place.

There were changes in both sides. The Ibrox side had Willie Henderson back on the right wing, but Jim Baxter was out with a knee injury kept secret until the last minute.

And Celtic had Jimmy Johnstone back! It has been another controversial start to the season for the fiery little right-winger. He had been left out of the pre-season games—apart from 45 minutes against Carlisle—and the opening League Cup games, in yet another attempt to try to impose a stricter discipline on him.

Still, there was a huge roar when his name was announced and he ran out for a match which would decide if the League Cup was to have a new home after its long spell at Parkhead.

And he played well in a game which finally ended in a narrow, but decisive, 1–0 victory for Celtic.

They had to wait until the second half for the goal, scored by Tommy Gemmell, from a twice-taken free-kick.

Willie Johnston had stood too near Bobby Murdoch at the first attempt, the ball had struck his arm, and referee Callaghan had ordered the second kick to be taken from where Johnston had been standing.

And from the second kick, Rangers' 'keeper, Gerry Neef, made a dreadful boob when he failed to catch it, and as he tried to snatch it again Gemmell nipped in to head it into the net.

Afterwards Tommy described it: 'Apart from penalties this was the first goal I have scored against Rangers . . . and what a way to get it! It was lovely to see the ball hit the back of the net.

'I positioned myself on the line in the hope that Bobby Murdoch's free-kick would come my way, and when Neef touched it on to me, all I had to do was stretch forward and net.

'It was not the most spectacular of goals, but it certainly is one I'll never forget.'

That goal virtually assured Celtic of a quarter-final place, for although they had the same number of points as Rangers, they had a superior goal difference.

There were no more slip-ups, they went on to beat Airdrie 3–0 at Broomfield, then Raith Rovers 5–2 at Kirkcaldy, while Rangers dropped another point in a draw with Raith at Ibrox.

But there was an unpleasant follow-up to the Parkhead game

Flat out . . . and in the League Cup Quarter Finals, that's left-back
Tommy Gemmell as he hits the Parkhead turf after heading Celtic's
winner against Rangers in a League Cup qualifying match

Now he's up, as team mate Bobby Lennox, with arms upstretched,
hails the Gemmell goal which gives their side victory

in which referee Jim Callaghan had booked three players: Celtic's Murdoch and Hughes, and McKinnon of Rangers.

Hughes had been booked towards the end of the first half, and soon after the interval he was involved in another incident when he retaliated after Johnston had kicked him in mid-field.

The referee, who was following play as it swung back up-field, did not see the clash, and it was a linesman who drew his attention to it.

After a long talk with Hughes, the big left-winger was allowed to stay on the field, although I personally considered the offence merited an ordering-off.

Two weeks later Rangers sent a letter of complaint to the S.F.A. about it. The Association's establishment closed ranks to order Mr. Callaghan to appear before the Referee Committee, and then suspended him for two months.

I felt the referee had made a mistake, but to pillory him by giving him a sentence which was heavier than players with considerable soccer crime records—and to put into doubt the very first principle that, right or wrong, a referee's decision is final—was a fierce decision indeed.

It was an unhappy episode, which ended with Celtic chairman, Sir Robert Kelly, resigning from the Referee Committee —he had not been at the meeting which sentenced the referee— and the S.F.A. Council, who would pass any motion of the establishment anyway, agreeing to the suspension.

But back to the field, where Celtic found they had no easy quarter-final task when they were drawn against Aberdeen.

The first game at Pittodrie ended in a hard-fought, no-scoring draw, and Celtic, without injured wingers Johnstone and Hughes, played an unusually tight 4–3–3 formation.

After this match manager Stein admitted: 'It has been the toughest opening spell I have known since returning to Celtic Park. This year there has been no break at all. We've been playing against all the teams we expected to make a real challenge.'

There was certainly no break in September in mid-week matches, for in between the two games against Aberdeen, Celtic packed in a trip to Basle for the opening European Cup match in Switzerland, with a 0–0 draw.

The second League Cup quarter-final drew 47,000 fans to Parkhead, and they were stunned in 31 minutes when centre Jim Forrest put Aberdeen ahead, and it could have been even worse when Dave Robb missed an excellent chance only minutes later.

46

Keep your eye on the ball . . . and the man illustrating one of football's golden rules is Celtic left-winger Bertie Auld as he waits for the header from Steve Chalmers, on the ground, to rebound to him for Celtic's goal in the League Cup Final against St. Johnstone

Salute to a goal . . . from Bertie Auld, Harry Hood and a high-jumping Steve Chalmers as they greet the goal which won yet another League Cup Final for Celtic

Yet again, as so often in a cup-tie, Celtic bounced back into a game, and in 52 minutes Bobby Lennox hit the equaliser and minutes later Willie Wallace picked up by a pass from Johnstone, was fouled by centre-half Tommy McMillan, stumbled, but regained his balance and ran on to score the eventual winner.

The semi-final was against Ayr United, the newly promoted babes of the First Division, and there were few in football who did not smile at manager Ally McLeod's pre-match prediction: 'I honestly think we can win.'

But they were not laughing at Ayr at the end, when it had taken an extra-time equaliser to save Celtic.

The League Cup holders had lined up without Jimmy Johnstone, who was ill, and Harry Hood had taken over from him on the right, and they had young Kenny Dalgleish at right-half.

Celtic got their first shock in 31 minutes when left-winger Bobby Rough put Ayr ahead, but four minutes later John Hughes equalised, and they seemed to be safely through when Gemell scored from a penalty in 50 minutes.

Left: The joy of winning . . . it's all mirrored in the face, and the actions, of Bertie Auld as he walks off Hampden at the end of the League Cup Final

Above: The prizes of winning . . . as a line of Celtic players, Billy McNeill, Bertie Auld and Harry Hood step up to receive the League Cup, and their victors' medals

But ten minutes later centre-forward Ingram snatched an equaliser, and the teams were tied at the end of 90 minutes.

Amazing Ayr swept into the lead at the start of extra time—thanks to Rough—and as Hampden wondered if it was watching a soccer sensation, it took a late and brilliant goal by substitute Bertie Auld to save Celtic.

You just could not keep these cheeky First Division newcomers down. for they scored first again in the replay, by centre Ingram.

However, Hood equalised; and in the second half Steve Chalmers pounced on a mistake by Skipper Stan Quinn to score the winner.

Sadly, Celtic's troubles were not over, for twelve minutes from time Ronnie Simpson made a brillian save—a save with all the hallmark of his class as a great goalkeeper—when he stopped a flick from Ingram which looked a certain equaliser.

49

Unfortunately he fell on the shoulder which he had injured the previous season and dislocated it again.

He had to be helped off, Gemmell took over in goal to hold out until the end . . . and Celtic were in their sixth successive League Cup Final.

The other finalists were St. Johnstone, who had shared in an exciting 2–2 draw with Celtic at Parkhead in the first game of the season.

No doubt the memory of that match attracted 73,000 fans to Hampden for the final . . . a game which was almost to be dwarfed by the happening off the field rather than on it.

Celtic sensationally left Tommy Gemmell out of the team, three days after he had been ordered off in the World Cup game between Scotland and West Germany.

There seemed no doubt that Celtic, always jealous of their reputation for field discipline, were taking a strong line again, despite the fact that it was a Cup Final.

The sequel was a transfer request from Gemmell the following day after a talk with Mr. Stein and Sir Robert Kelly.

Yet on the field it was a marvellous game for that remarkable veteran Bertie Auld, playing only his third full game of the season, and scoring his side's winner in their 1–0 victory after just two minutes.

There was also an effective come-back from Bobby Murdoch, who was appearing in the first team again after his absence on a weight-reducing course at a health farm.

So Celtic wrapped up four major domestic trophies, in six months, and that's not likely to happen again.

They had been helped by a twist of the soccer calendar. The previous season's League Cup Final had been held over because of the Hampden fire until April, then that month came the Scottish Cup Final and the League Championship, and in October they successfully defended the League Cup again.

It had been quite a start to the season!

The Greatest Goalscorer

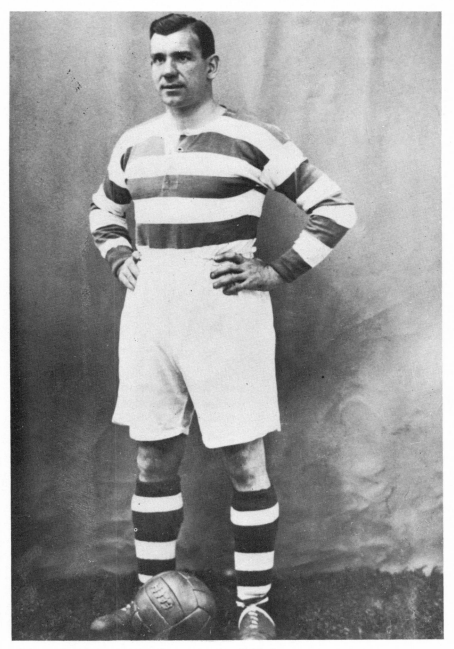

A picture to jog the memory of every pre-war Celtic fan . . .
centre-forward Jimmy McGrory stands, for once at ease, in the strip
which made him Britain's most feared soccer scoring machine

His name needs no preliminary flourishes, no false fanfares, for he long ago carved his way into Scottish football history . . . and the place of Jimmy McGrory among the soccer giants is secure for ever.

The statistic that won James Edward McGrory his way into football's hall of fame sounds so simple to say—550 goals in his career from 1923 to 1937—but is still almost incredible to comprehend by a modern generation reared on defensive tactics aimed at blotting out attackers.

I must declare my interest straight away, before I upset any older readers who may lovingly cherish memories of watching McGrory in his hey-day.

I never saw him play, indeed I was not even born by the time he had retired from his long spell as Celtic's number nine.

However, all football memories are not just instant history, and in preparing this chapter I have been fascinated by the look back to the era of the 'Golden Twenties', of a Celtic ruled by Willie Maley and Rangers by Bill Struth . . . the giants who battled then, just as the clubs still do in the seventies, for the supremacy of Scottish football.

As the sounds of a new Celtic generation echoed from a practice match on the car park outside, I talked recently to Jimmy McGrory in the Parkhead board-room, decorated by so many of the lovingly-cared-for trophies he had helped to win.

The famous pipe—his trade-mark as a manager—waved in his hand as he told me modestly: 'I'm not much good at these interviews looking back.'

But the stocky little man, his shoulders and brow still as broad as the days when he was heading his way to a goals record, proved himself wrong as he spun me back to the days of names that still conjure excitement, though some, alas, are dead, and it's decades since any of them last kicked a ball in competition.

Names such as Patsy Gallacher and John Thomson, or the eternal Ibrox opposition from such men as Bob McPhail and Alan Morton.

No computer could have answered more convincingly the question I put to Jimmy McGrory about the difference between present-day football and those days forty years ago when he was the hero of the Parkhead terracing.

How would he have managed in today's fiercely defensive football . . . could he still have created scoring records?

The answer was as firmly placed as any goal he ever scored . . . 'I have no doubt I would not have got even half the

The fashion styles have changed . . . but cup winning was just as much a target for Celtic in 1931—when this picture was taken after they had beaten Motherwell—as it will be in 1971. Jimmy McGrory is second from the left in the bottom row—next to skipper Jimmy McStay—both of them were eventually to manage the club

number. I feel sorry for the modern forward with all he has to combat from modern defensive methods.

'I salute a player such as George Best when he scores six goals; even if it is against an English Fourth Division side it is still a marvellous feat in today's defensive conditions.'

Strangely enough, three times at the beginning of his career the pairing of the man and the club, McGrory of Celtic, which is now inseparable, almost failed to come about.

Although he came from the Garngad area of Glasgow—a stronghold of Parkhead fans—and played for one of Celtic's great nursery sides, St. Roch's, he did not immediately fancy joining the club.

Then he was inside-right and the holder of the position was Patsy Gallacher, and no youngster could possibly imagine taking over from that hero of heroes.

Third Lanark wanted him, too, but then, as in later years, the financial affairs of the Cathkin club stopped them moving for the player.

However, at 17 Celtic managed to overcome all his fears, and on 20 January 1923 he made his first-team début at Cathkin—at inside-right in place of the injured Gallacher—but Third Lanark marred it somewhat by winning 1–0.

But it was in his third game, on 3 February 1923, that the first of the long, long line of goals, which was to stretch to over five hundred, was scored.

It was in a League match against Kilmarnock at Rugby Park, and after ten minutes a shot from left-winger Adam McLean was blocked, and McGrory nipped in to score, the first goal in a 4–3 victory.

But later that year he was farmed out to Clydebank, then newly promoted to the First Division, and managed by the old Celtic star, Jimmy Hay.

'I was told I was going to gain experience, but quite honestly I thought they were getting rid of me in a nice way,' he told me.

The Clydebank chairman went on record as saying: 'I hope Celtic forget all about this laddie,' but the laddie soon made sure that was impossible.

McGrory scored his first hat-trick in an 8–2 Scottish Cup victory against Blairgowrie on 26 January 1924 . . . and in March he returned to Parkhead for a League match, still a Clydebank player.

He was now outside-left, and it was the sort of homecoming which seems now to belong to dust-covered copies of boys' magazines, for he scored an equaliser, and Clydebank went on to beat Celtic 2–1.

Not surprisingly, that was the beginning of the end of his time with Clydebank. A couple of months later he was back at Parkhead where the rest of his career in football, apart from a spell with Kilmarnock as manager, was to be spent.

And, within a few weeks of his return, he had won his first honour with Celtic, a Charity Cup-Winners medal, after his first-ever 'Old Firm' match.

It was played at Hampden, the first goal scored by Patsy Gallacher, the equaliser by Alan Morton, and the winner by Willie McStay . . . all men who were giants of their era.

Curiously, he returned to Celtic Park for £4 a week, a pound less than he had been earning with Clydebank. And, in fact, he told me that his wage averaged out at no more than £7 a week during his entire playing career . . . what a pittance it seems beside today's executive-size salaries!

So, the start of the McGrory legend was forged! Naturally, even then, supporters compared the stars of that era with the pre-First World War players.

Was McGrory as good as the legendary Jimmy Quinn?

Celtic chairman Tom White supplied the answer . . . 'There will never be another Jimmy Quinn. But I tell you what we do have, a Jimmy McGrory.'

The records were soon falling. In February 1927 he beat the Scottish League record for goals in a season—which then stood at 43—by scoring four goals against St. Mirren at Parkhead . . . and jubilant fans carried him shoulder-high to the pavilion.

The following year in a League match against Dunfermline at Parkhead he smashed the individual scoring record of six goals in a First Division game, by totting up eight against the Fifers, a record which still stands . . . and not one of them was scored with his head!

It was at the end of that season that Arsenal, set to become the greatest English side of the thirties, made their famous bid for McGrory.

Nearly 42 years later he recalled the moves when he said. 'Three times, Herbert Chapman (who was then the Arsenal manager) tried to sign me. But I never had any desire to move, and I never regretted it.

'I suppose the club were short of money at the time, and that's why they wanted me to go.

A look back down memory lane . . . as Jimmy McGrory, then manager, talks with some of the men who helped to win the honours of the 'fifties, *left to right*, Jock Stein, Charlie Tully, Bobby Evans, Sean Fallon, Bobby Collins, Bertie Peacock and Neil Mochan

'I asked Mr. Chapman once, during the negotiations, what the fee was for me, but he just smiled and said it would not be fair to disclose it.

'Some people said it was a blank cheque, others said it was £10,000; maybe that would be the equivalent of £100,000 today . . . I just don't know.

'It meant that I would have got only around £200 from the transfer, and I decided to stay. I honestly never had any desire to move. There was, and certainly still is, something about Celtic that made them different; few players ever wanted to leave.

'Some people says it's religious, but that's just rubbish. I think it's more of a family atmosphere, and it's always been like that.'

Then, on 21 December 1931, came the goal he now describes as the best he ever scored; naturally, it was a header.

The match was against Aberdeen, and his goals total stood at 361 goals . . . one short of the then British record held by Hughie Ferguson of Motherwell and Cardiff.

How many players can you recall from these teams? Celtic: Kennoway, Hogg, McGonagle; Morrison, Lyon, Paterson; Fagan, Buchan, McGrory, Crum, Murphy.

Aberdeen: Smith, Cooper, McGill; Fraser, Falloon, Thomson; Warnock, McKenzie, Armstrong, Mills, Lang.

He had equalled the record in seven minutes with the first goal of the game, but after Aberdeen equalised he had gone off injured when he clashed with 'keeper Smith and injured his back on the frozen ground.

Soon after, he returned to bullet a cross from Frank Murphy into the net to set up a new record, but apparently it had not been too accurate a cross and one writer described it: 'There was not a centre living that day who could have scored, except McGrory.'

Just to wrap things up neatly he scored a hat-trick, in a match which Celtic finally won 5–2.

It was also at that time that one of football's greatest-ever tragedies occurred when Celtic 'keeper John Thomson died as the result of an accident in a match against Rangers at Ibrox.

Jimmy McGrory told me: 'He was not only the greatest goalkeeper I have ever seen, but the most natural athlete. He could have starred in any sport.

'I remember not long after he joined us we were all at Seamill and we discovered he could not swim. I jumped into the pool, and shouted to him to join us.

'Most beginners would have jumped in feet first, but he executed the most wonderful dive you could ever want to see.

'Another sport he didn't know anything about at first was golf. He used to caddy for myself or Johnny McFarlane, and sometimes Willie McStay.

'I was amazed he could not play golf, coming from Fife. So one day I said to him to have a try.

'And he just stood there and hit a perfect drive, and followed it up with another second shot.'

The man who is now Celtic's public relations officer drew on his pipe and said reflectively: 'Thank God there are few accidents as bad as that in football. But what a pity it had to be him; he was so young.'

Step forward now to October 1937, and the last time Jimmy McGrory was to wear the famous green-and-white hooped jersey of Celtic.

The season before, he had scored his highest number of goals in one season, but as he explained to me: 'I knew that it was

The end and the beginning of a Celtic era. It's March 1965, and new boss Jock Stein stands with the man who was once his manager at Parkhead, Jimmy McGrory

becoming harder to chase after balls. Passes that a few years earlier I had caught with ease had become an effort.'

Kilmarnock had made an offer to him to join them as manager. His boss, Willie Maley, told him to turn it down, but one director advised him to accept . . . 'You never know where it might lead,' were his prophetic words.

So, after 410 League goals, the total swollen to 550 with Cup and international matches, seven full and six League caps, five Scottish Cup medals, two League championship awards, and several Glasgow Cup and Charity Cup medals, he stepped off soccer's stage as a player.

And, of course, by 1946 he was back as manager of Celtic to lead them to honours in the Scottish Cup, League Cup, League championship, Coronation Cup, St. Mungo Cup, Glasgow Cup and Charity Cup.

Then, in 1965, he moved over to become the club's first-ever public relations officer, and Jock Stein was appointed the new manager.

There was not a trace of bitterness about the move, none of the nastiness so often associated with these changes in one of the most ruthless jobs in any industry.

His eyes twinkled as he quipped: 'I retired at 60. When I look around now I'm sure it won't be long before managers retire at 50.' And who is to say he is wrong?

McGrory as a player and manager spans nearly 50 years in football, and of today's high-speed football he says: 'There is no doubt it's played far quicker today.

'The styles have changed completely. I don't look back with regret. But I do feel a bit sorry that in some teams the individuals have given way to team plans. You used to be able to look at teams outside the "Old Firm" and they always had a couple of players who were individual attractions; I don't think that happens so much today.'

Yet, behind all the awards, all the honours, there is something much rarer about Jimmy McGrory. He is that phenomenon in football, a man who has no enemies.

When he was ill three years ago with a heart attack, one of his visitors in hospital was Rangers' chairman, John Lawrence. . . . I wonder what the mobs who besmirch 'Old Firm' games would have made of that!

And today, at Celtic Park, every member of the staff, his successor Jock Stein, the players from captain Billy McNeill down to the youngest boot-boy, still address him by the accolade: 'Boss'!

The Italian Campaign

Number one in Europe . . . there's no doubt that's what Tommy
Gemmell, Bertie Auld and Willie Wallace think Celtic should be
called, as they prepare to fly home after the victory against
Fiorentina. And if you think there's something cardboard about the
smile of the air hostess—you're right. She's a cardboard cut-out

THE big man, his grey coat flapping in the night drizzle as he limped on to the pitch of the Stadio Communale in Florence, headed straight for Jimmy Johnstone . . . to totally engulf his little winger in a massive bear hug of congratulations.

Celtic had just been beaten 1–0 by the Italian champions in the quarter-final of the European Cup—but they had cruised into the semi-final spot with 3–1 aggregate victory—and Jock Stein had every reason for the melon-sized grin which split his face.

The bitterness of the memory of that last round, when—with a similar situation of a three-goal lead from the first leg—they had lost it to Benfica in Lisbon and then had to depend on a toss of a coin for victory, all that had been eased at last.

This time the opposition had met their masters, and the Italian crowd knew it. When Celtic lined up in the middle of the stadium for the now traditional end of the match wave to the crowd, applause swept the ground from the fans, in stark contrast to the hostility they had shown at the start.

It had been another magnificent first for Celtic to add to their lengthy collection of honours. There was no trophy to collect this time, but the record books will record it as just as important.

For it was the first time a British side had ever triumphed against an Italian team over two legs in the fifteen-year history of the European Cup.

And it has been done in the classic tactical way by Celtic with the plans laid down by their manager . . . attack at home, defend away.

When the draw had been made away back in December, and they had been paired with Fiorentina, Stein had remarked: 'Playing against a Latin team is always exciting. They have that bit of extra glamour, and obviously they are a good side. You have to be to win the Italian League.'

The quarter-finals of the European Cup have the longest lapse between the actual draw and the games. So long that, when they first heard in December they were playing Fiorentina, Celtic were not even top of the Scottish First Division, but when the tie was over by March, they were seven points ahead of their nearest rivals, Rangers.

Stein had wasted no time in making the first spy jaunt to see Fiorentina. Even although weather delayed him on his way to Florence, he saw them draw with Roma, managed by his old adversary, Helenio Herrera, former boss of Inter-Milan.

The Italian coach, Bruno Pesaola, a swarthy little man with

enormous black eyebrows delayed his look at Celtic until only ten days before the first leg of the tie at Parkhead.

The match he picked was the Scottish Cup quarter-final against Rangers at Parkhead, the 'Old Firm' battle of the giants which Celtic finally won 3–1 after one of the seasons' most bruising, bitter battles.

I believe it scared him stiff! Managers are always cagey about what they say after these spy trips, any careless talk that it will be easy for their side has a nasty habit of rebounding.

There were no forecasts from Pesaola, but he said unhappily: 'I am very worried. It was so tough. I had not imagined it would be like that and, in Italy, at least five men would have been sent off.'

However after Fiorentina had lost the first leg 3–0 their manager claimed: 'Whoever ventures into a wild circus such as that Glasgow stadium jammed by a partisan crowd has a right to be afraid.'

Just to make sure . . . a delighted Bobby Lennox follows the ball into the net after it has bounced off a Fiorentina defender for Celtic's second goal

I am convinced that he was really talking about the 'Old Firm' match and not the actual European Cup game, for he also said: 'My players had stiff legs, and lost their concentration and determination before walking into the game.' And that was before the match!

It could only have been because he had perhaps communicated too well to his players the atmosphere of an 'Old Firm' Cup-tie—thankfully a unique brand of fan fervour—for the crowd at the game against Fiorentina were, for some of the match, quieter than I have heard.

Jock Stein had taken his final look at Fiorentina the Sunday before the game in Glasgow, when they lost 1–0 away to Torino.

Still, the friendly Italians offered him a lift in their charter plane from Italy to Scotland, and Stein—no doubt with memories of his team's shock league defeat by Hearts before the Benfica game—said: 'I am not paying much attention to the result. I know how a European Cup match can take up a team's full attention.'

The Italians had a shock absentee from their side, right-winger Luciano Chiarugi, who had been left at home apparently because of a leg injury, although the Italian press hinted darkly at club discipline.

There seemed some substance to these reports when the player broke his silence to say: 'Pesaola cannot treat me like this. I would have been fit to play in Scotland.'

All managers of Italian sides wave their arms about during press interviews and tell you, without the slightest trace of a blush, that theirs is an attacking team.

Pesaola had more reason than most, however, to have his statement accepted for his team had won the Italian championship with attacking football.

So he settled in at his Troon headquarters, and expansively said: 'My team is an attacking team. I do not like the Italian defensive style of play.'

Alas for him, his words were proved to be yet another soccer equivalent of a smoke-screen . . . and they were to cause him not a little concern after the Parkhead game.

Celtic lined up with a team of: Williams; Hay, Gemmell; Murdoch, McNeill, Brogan; Johnstone, Lennox, Wallace, Auld, Hughes. The shock inclusion was Bertie Auld, who had not played in the first team because of an injury for nearly six weeks.

But was it really a shock? As Leeds United boss Don Revie joked on television later: 'Jock just keeps Auld for these European Cup games.'

Bertie admitted later: 'Forty minutes before the game I went out to give some relatives tickets. I told them I didn't know if I was playing. Then I went back to the dressing-room, and the manager told me I was in the team.'

It was a vintage Auld performance that night. Waving his arms about, like an angry traffic cop, he repeatedly picked the ball up in mid-field and gave instructions to his team-mates on the positions they should take up to beat the purple-shirted barrier of Fiorentina.

The man who had to hurl his way through the gaps was left-winger John Hughes. This was a brave performance by Hughes, chopped down repeatedly by right-back Rogora . . . the fiercest defender I have seen since the bitter methods of Racing Club in the world championship.

Celtic orbited into the attack in the blast-off style which has become their trademark. Only inches stopped them grabbing that first, and all-important goal. Then, just perhaps when their impetus was beginning to wear a little thin, they struck.

A move between Bobby Murdoch and John Hughes, and it was Auld who found a gap at last in that Fiorentina defence with a long, low shot to score.

Two minutes after half time, and when Harry Hood had substituted for the injured Hughes, it was Auld again . . . this time a cross from the left which cannoned off Carpenetti and into the net.

Predictably Auld, after his absence, began to tire after that, and as the Italians closed their ranks even further the Celtic attack got caught in a defensive web.

There was a stream of instructions from the dug-out. The full-backs, Hay and Gemmell, were switched, Jock Stein even walked round the track to pass on instructions to his men.

Just as the fans were getting restive, some of them around me even talking nervously about a Fiorentina breakaway, the match-winning adrenalin magically surged through Celtic again.

It was Auld—who else?—who crossed the ball from the left, Hood headed back across the goal and Wallace completed the move to score.

The difference one goal can make in Europe was never better illustrated than on that cold March night. Two goals of a lead from a first-leg is no longer safe . . . three, despite Benfica, should be enough for any side.

The anxious murmurs changed to a full-throated chorus of adulation as the Celtic manager pushed his side back on to the park to receive the crowd's ovation.

Proudly Stein said the next day: 'Do you realise what happened out there last night? They have their million-lire transfer fees, their £60,000 a year coaches, a football fanaticism which is almost a religion.

'Yet with all their resources we licked them. It was not just a great night for Celtic, it was a wonderful advert for Scottish football.'

Predictably it was another story for Pesaola. He returned home to find a storm of criticism breaking over him from the Italian press and at the next home games banners demanding his sacking were waved by angry fans, for, to add to his worries, the game had been seen live on Italian television.

He admitted then: 'It is true we did not go to Glasgow to win, but to keep the score at reasonable terms, or with some luck, grab a draw.

'I only played the same way as any other Italian team. A.C. Milan were lucky to get a victory in Glasgow against Celtic last season, when they played defensive, but everyone hailed them as heroes.'

That was a slightly slanted view, for the A.C. Milan defensive set-up was superior to Fiorentina, and they also had a forward such at Prati who could make a goal out of barely half a chance, something of which Pesaola's side never seemed capable.

The press were not the most important people to whom Pesaola had to make explanations. He was closetted with his club directors for an hour after the Parkhead game . . . and I don't expect the atmosphere in the dressing-room was any warmer, for it was obvious that the much-publicised bonus of £1,500 per man which Fiorentina had offered their players for the tie almost disappeared.

Yet, even with these three goals, there was still the memory of Lisbon in the previous round hovering over Celtic.

The same situation, a second leg away from home, the same score. Would the unthinkable happen again?

Not if Jock Stein had anything to do with it!

A week before the second leg he told me of his battle plans, they involved a complete change in Celtic's pre-match pattern.

The usual plan is to discuss the game at some convenient time, perhaps the day before or even the day of the game. This time it was to be different.

The soccer talk-in started at 11 a.m. on the Sunday before the match . . . the final briefing was at 11 a.m. three days later on Wednesday, the day of the game.

Left: Two to one . . . but another Fiorentina attack collapses as Celtic right-back David Hay efficiently clears the danger

Right: One man against a team . . . face screwed in concentration, Willie Wallace chases after the ball on one of those lung-searing runs to take the pressure off his own defence in Florence

An Italian spy would have given a lot to know what was said on the second-floor lounge of Celtic's hotel high above the hills of Florence, as Stein, in a grey cardigan, gathered his green track-suited players around him to go over, yet again, their battle plans.

His cutting commentary on the near-disaster of Benfica had been: 'A combination of carelessness, lack of concentration and trying to be too clever.'

But when he confided his pre-match plans and I watched the match, it was like seeing a book transformed into a film, you almost knew what was coming next.

He had said Jimmy Johnstone could be an ace up front—and he was! He had said the mid-field was the key to the game and if defenders were needed there it would be a recognised defender who would play . . . George Connelly was the shock choice at right-half!

The image of Celtic is of swashbuckling, attack all the time, a team whose style is loved by fans wherever they see it.

The more intricate, concentrated defensive planning upset some of their fans who felt it was tactics which the side never seemed at ease operating.

Stein countered that by saying that two of the most professional performances the team had given in Europe had been the year before in Europe . . . a 1–1 draw in Belgrade against Red Star and, more important in view of the fact that they were going back to Italy, a 0–0 draw against A.C. Milan in the San Siro Stadium.

And he told me: 'I would be happy with a draw in Florence. I am not going there to boast about what Celtic will do in the game. I'm going simply not to lose, and to get through to the semi-finals.'

Only the result was wrong in his pre-match predictions. A 1–0 defeat, but that could be forgiven in the general elation of the aggregate victory.

The team read: Williams; Hay, Gemmell; Connelly, McNeill, Brogan; Johnstone, Murdoch, Wallace, Lennox, Auld.

What an incredible change for young Connelly. Only six days before, on a dismally cold Thursday, I had slipped into Parkhead to take a look at Stein's starlets of tomorrow's Celtic.

They had won easily against Dundee United and Connelly had time—perhaps too much time for a centre-half—to show the few fans in the crowd some of his undoubted ball control.

Yet less than a week later he was coping magnificently with all the pressures of a European Cup quarter-final, in the country with some of the world's most partisan football fans. All the traces of the casual soccer of the reserve side vanished as he set out to control the middle of the park with Billy McNeill.

The Celtic players had been so well briefed they had even been told that if they were upfield, and thought they had no chance of scoring or no team-mate to whom they could pass, not to just try a speculative shot at the keeper.

They were to hit the ball deliberately over the bar to allow the team to reform, they were not all to be caught out upfield.

There were two extremely anxious moments in the first half. Once when right-winger Chiarugi—restored to the side by Pesaola—shot in directly from a free-kick. Fortunately the rockets had scarcely risen joyfully from the Italian fans on the terracing before they realised, as it was an indirect free-kick, it was no goal, for it had touched no other player.

Fiorentina scored their goal in 36 minutes, after one of the decisions of Swiss referee Rudolf Scheurer, some of which were so odd that Stein snapped at the end: 'Everything was

The goal that really knocked Italian champions Fiorentina out of the
European Cup . . . the last-minute header by Willie Wallace which
made it 3—0 for Celtic at Parkhead

for the Italians. I am not surprised that British teams find it
almost impossible to win in Italy.'

The referee took Billy McNeill's name for his first foul of
the game and one that seemed merely technical. McNeill,
sensing the danger, dashed back to his position as the Italians
quickly took the free-kick, and chipped the ball into the centre.

The big centre-half, who had one of his most magnificent
matches in his long career, was just in time to head the ball
but, caught off balance, he could only half turn it in the penalty
area, and Chiarugi fastened on to it to score.

Was it ominous for Celtic? It was almost the same time as
the first goal in Lisbon. I must admit I felt a chill of appre-
hension.

Pesaola, who spent almost all the first half leaping off his
seat on the trainer's bench to encourage his side, nearly became
Italy's first spaceman as he bobbed up and down with joy.

However, it was to be his one real moment of happiness. There was no collapse this time, the nearest was a low shot from Chiarugi in the second half which hit the post and spun back into the hands of Williams.

The most bizarre moment did come in the second half when the referee gave a free kick against Celtic when their defenders were passing back too often to their own 'keeper from just outside the penalty box.

Despite press probing at the end, it was a mystery which was never satisfactorily solved, for the referee took refuge in a rule which was unknown to the Scots.

Perhaps the fans of Fiorentina did not see the real Celtic. But they had one consolation, they saw Jimmy Johnstone!

This was one of his finest matches. Too often he has reserved his best performances in Europe for his own Parkhead, and contributed little when the team went abroad.

It was different in Florence. For often he was the only forward upfield, especially in the second half when he was switched to centre, and Willie Wallace moved to the right-wing to stop left-back Longoni coming through.

It must have been impossible, even for the watching telly fans back home, because of TV's concentration on the man on the ball, to appreciate Johnstone's performance.

At times the little red-head had a posse of purple-shirted Italians waiting to stop him. Yet he stuck grimly to his task.

However, it was Bobby Murdoch that Fiorentina coach Pesaola spotlighted when he told me: 'Murdoch is the papa of the team. The rest are the sons around him.'

Yet after the match, as I made my way back from the ground, strap-hanging on a number eleven bus, I did not need fluent Italian to make out how often the fans were talking about Johnstone.

He even won a huge roar from the crowd when it was all over, and he presented his jersey to a ball-boy, a neat public relations job that the Johnstone of even a few years ago would not have thought about.

But these defenders around Johnstone had proved Stein right. For the Italians, committed week by week to stale defence in their League programme, did not move up centre-half Ferrante to help out their attack, even when time was rapidly running out on them.

It was a fact that was not lost on the Italian press. As Stein stood outside the dressing-room door holding the traditional end-of-the-match press conference, one perceptive local reporter asked him what he would have done with Ferrante in a similar

Salute of victory . . . as the Celtic players acknowledge the homage
of their fans after the victory against Fiorentina

situation. He was politely told that the problem was Pesaola's
. . . not Celtic's.

But the psychology of Stein did not extend just to men on
the park. Sitting on the bench, although not as substitutes,
were two of his reserves, David Cattenach and Victor Davidson.

They were on the trip, not just to absorb the special atmosphere of a European Cup match, and not just to learn from
the moves of such experienced European masters as Bertie Auld
or Billy McNeill.

'I wanted them to see Connelly and Hay out there. They have
played in the reserves with them. I wanted them to think "If
they can play in a European tie, so can I",' said the manager.

So that, even in Florence, the future for Stein did not stretch
just as far as the semi-finals . . . but extended to European
campaigns none of us have even thought about yet.

My Dream Transfer

I NEVER spot people in a crowd at a League match. As you can imagine, I have far too much on my mind to try to recognise familiar faces.

But it is different at a reserve game. Usually on the terracing there is only a handful of fans, and it is easier to pick out someone whom you may know.

However, I must admit it is a rare occurrence even at a reserve fixture . . . but the day it happened to me it changed my entire football career.

It was at a reserve match between Wolves and Liverpool at Molineux about eighteen months ago. Suddenly, during a break in the play, my Wolves team-mate, Francis Munro moved up beside me and muttered: 'Take a look behind your goal when you can. I'm sure that's Sean Fallon standing there.'

I took a peep round, and sure enough it was the Celtic assistant manager, who had paid his way on to the terraces . . . although I was so surprised I had a second look just to make sure.

The only two Scots on the field were Francis Munro and myself. By the way, my Welsh-sounding name is my only connection with Wales.

As I knew Celtic were looking for a 'keeper, I wondered if perhaps it was me he was watching; however, as time went on I heard nothing more about a transfer to Scotland, and I began to think that the Celtic interest had evaporated.

And, in fact, the next transfer I was involved in was to another English club . . . I went on loan from Wolves to their Midland neighbours, Aston Villa, on a two-month contract.

The manager then was the mercurial Tommy Docherty, who later left Villa mid-way through the season. However, when the time came for my temporary contract to expire, the Doc wanted to make it a permanent transfer, and he offered me a two-year contract at Villa Park, with a two-year option.

I was undecided about it, so I decided to have a talk with Wolves' manager, Billy McGarry, about the situation before I finally made up my mind.

As we sat in his office discussing the Villa bid, he asked me if I was still keen to return to Scotland, for one of the clubs there had been asking about me.

A high-flying save from 'keeper Evan Williams as he punches away
the ball from Aberdeen centre Jim Forrest in the Scottish Cup Final

Finally he revealed it was Celtic. I just could not believe it;
I thought he was joking. However, he put through a call to
Glasgow to try to contact Mr. Stein, but unfortunately he was
not available at that moment.

So, to pass the time, I decided to join the reserves at a training
session. I was just about to step on to the track when I was
called back to Mr. McGarry's office.

It was Mr. Stein on the phone. He asked me if I could catch
the first train north, which left Wolverhampton at 11.30 a.m.
. . . and it was not far off that time by then!

I dashed back to the dressing-room to change again. I'll
never forget the look of amazement on the faces of Francis

Munro and Derek Dougan. They thought that perhaps some of my family in Scotland had been taken ill when I gasped that I was rushing for the Glasgow ,train . . . they just would not believe that I was going to sign for Celtic.

I sped out of Molineux for the last time, after the most breath-taking thirty minutes of my career, which had changed the course of my football future entirely.

So instead of an Aston Villa player I was going to be Celtic player, and that's how it worked out. But I will always be grateful to Bill McGarry for allowing me the chance. He had told me that if a Scots club ever came along for me he would not stand in my way, and Wolves would only take a nominal transfer fee.

Naturally neither of us ever imagined it would be the top Scottish club who would want me. But it did not change his attitude . . . he kept his promise.

Perhaps some fans have wondered why I should succeed with Celtic when, I must admit, I was no great success in England.

They said the same thing in England about Bertie Auld, after his great achievement with Celtic when he came home from Birmingham City, although Bertie's spell down south was more successful than mine, maybe it's another part of the Parkhead magic.

In my case I was signed by Wolves from Third Lanark to be one of the reserve 'keepers at Molineux, and I am afraid I could never quite overcome that tag.

After only three months I asked away, then things did improve and I got a run in the first team—one of my games was against Manchester United and the man I consider to have one of the most dangerous shots in English football, Bobby Charlton.

But it was soon back to reserve football. For I am convinced that in English football today, if you are transferred—and it's not for a huge sum—you can be disregarded very quickly.

There had been other clubs after me before I got the chance to join Aston Villa. I used to discuss it with my wife for hours, but I never fancied moving into the Third or Fourth Divisions of the English League.

I always felt that if I could get the right move I would be ready to grasp the opportunity, although never in my wildest dreams did I imagine it would be Celtic.

I am not bitter about English football. But don't believe all the propaganda that is peddled about how backward Scottish football is compared to the soccer down south.

Players can succeed in Scotland who have not starred in

The agony . . . as a cross from the right zooms across the face of the
Celtic goal, and goes on to hit right-back Jim Craig and bounce
past his own 'keeper, Evan Williams, for Rangers only goal in the
Scottish Cup match at Parkhead

English football. But it's not necessarily because the standard
is higher there.

I have found a tremendous difference since I came back,
and the training methods Celtic use for my own position is
just one example.

They are far ahead of any manager I worked under in
England. Take Tommy Docherty, for example. I've a great
admiration for the 'Doc'. I think he's the complete football
fanatic, and that's not a bad thing for any manager.

But I never agreed with him on his training methods for
'keepers. I would not make a good out-field player. I'm not
a great runner; Bobby Lennox does not need to worry about
me challenging him.

However, at Aston Villa I did the full out-field players'
schedule, and then the specialised 'keeper training. The result
was that when I came to the part which should have done me
the most good, I was exhausted.

Yet I must admit there were times in the first few weeks at

Parkhead when I felt I was a complete flop; I even wondered if I had made the right decision.

Gradually that specialised training which Mr. Stein gives his 'keeper began to pay off. I had one weakness in my game—I'm not going to give away any trade secrets—but the manager never said anything to me about it.

He just kept plugging away at it in training until he remarked one day: 'You don't like that.' And then he took me aside to show me how to sort it out.

Looking back, I am grateful that I was not pitchforked into the League team. I was allowed to get used to my new surroundings, my new training schedule, and adjust myself before I was given my chance.

The biggest shock I got was when I was told I would be playing in the League match against Rangers at Parkhead on 3 January . . . only thirty minutes before the kick-off!

I had never imagined I would be selected for that match, so I did not have time to get any real pre-match nerves.

Everyone at Celtic Park has been wonderful to me since I joined the club. For I must admit I was a bit worried about how the rest of the lads, who have won so many trophies—they never tire of telling me that—would react to a newcomer.

I need not have had any fears. When I first went to the ground the only player who was there from the first-team pool was Bobby Murdoch. I knew him from my previous spell in Scotland, and I mentioned these fears.

I always remember him saying: 'Don't worry. The lads will get to know you, before you even know them.'

One player who has been particularly helpful is Ronnie Simpson. Believe me, it's only now that I have had a spell as Celtic 'keeper that I appreciate just how well he did during his magnificent spell.

One problem facing a Celtic 'keeper, which you can apply to few other teams, is that there is rarely constant pressure. Maybe you think that should make life easier . . . but in fact in some ways it's harder.

It's always best for a 'keeper to be where the action is, keeping his eye in constantly with a string of saves.

I sometimes go two, or even three games with really not all that much to do. Then suddenly you have to guard against a snap breakaway to stop the opposition scoring, and ruining all your team-mates' attacking efforts.

It's a question of keeping your concentration on the game to be ready for anything. That's why I run around my penalty area a lot of the time when play is at the other end of the field.

I also shout instructions to my team-mates but, although 'keepers are supposed to be daft, I have not just got to the stage of talking to myself yet.

I know I have to keep my mind on the game. Fortunately in many ways I am my own biggest critic. For I consider you should treat every move in the match with respect.

It's a bit like golf. If you can cut out stupid mistakes, then you immediately lower your score. Of course the player who never made a mistake has not yet been born.

But if a 'keeper really works to cut down his quota of mistakes, then obviously he reduces the chances of losing stupid goals.

I like to be a little nervous, too, before a match. I find it helps me to have a better game, and one match I was certainly edgy about was the second leg of the European Cup quarter-final against Fiorentina in Italy.

I could hardly sleep for three days before the match for thinking about it, as it was the first game I had played for the team abroad. However, it worked out well, for although we were beaten 1–0 in Florence, we won on a 3–1 aggregate.

The sweat of training . . . as Evan Williams gets into the routine during his first training session after he joined Celtic

As I have told you, I notice a great difference in the standard of football in Scotland now, compared to the time I was with Third Lanark.

I think Celtic's 1967 European Cup victory was the best shot in the arm Scottish soccer ever had, for it swept aside the feeling that we were always destined to be second best.

Every team does not have the resources of Celtic. But more teams than ever are working hard, plotting and planning to try to topple the big sides, and that can't be a bad thing—even although I hope their victories against us are few and far between.

My previous club was Third Lanark and, although they often struggled before they finally went out of existence, I enjoyed playing with them . . . perhaps because I had never known anything else.

Now I find it hard to believe that I am playing in the same League, the professional standards have risen so much.

Perhaps Third Lanark's constant financial worries contributed to that. Money was always tight at Cathkin, and it was never shown better than on one trip north we made to Aberdeen.

We had been relegated to the Second Division and, because we had a blank Saturday on our fixture list, a match had been arranged against Aberdeen Reserves when we played our full League side.

It's a long way back from Aberdeen to Glasgow and on the road home we imagined we would be stopping at a restaurant for a meal.

However, we rolled on in the mini-bus towards Glasgow, and when finally we did stop, a club official handed us our 'tea money' . . . enough for one fish supper each!

That was life at Cathkin; I can look back now and have a good laugh at it. The reason I joined them in the first place was, for the very good one, that they were the only club who made me a signing offer.

When I was with Vale of Leven juniors, I had played almost half-a-dozen trials for various senior clubs, but I got so fed up with these trials that I decided I would play no more . . . until I got a definite signing offer.

So when Thirds came along I accepted their terms. Later the manager, Mr. Bill Hiddlestone was always telling me Celtic were interested in my transfer, but I never found out if it was true or not.

And I had to wait a few more years for the dream I had cherished, to play for the Parkhead club, to come true.

Five Flags in a Row

That champagne feeling . . . as Tommy Gemmell leads the celebrations in the bath at Tynecastle after Celtic clinched the championship

Six years ago a League championship flag for Celtic might have seemed as remote as a man walking on the moon. It was something that was always promised, but always apparently belonged to the future.

Celtic finished season 1964–65 tucked in an unspectacular eighth position, thirteen points behind the League champions, Willie Waddell's Kilmarnock.

But, by April 1970, they had wrapped up their fifth successive League championship, and finished twelve points ahead of Willie Waddell's Rangers, the biggest margin of the battle for the championship which had been fought between the two clubs.

77

Yet I had the feeling that last season too many people tended almost to underwrite the championship victory, as if it were by right it should go to Celtic.

Perhaps it was because the last lap, so often a nerve-straining fight to the finish, was so much a foregone football conclusion. Perhaps it was because the championship became overshadowed by the European Cup semi-finals against Leeds United.

But it is well to remember that League flags were once a rarity at Parkhead. The 1966 victory, for instance—the first of that famous five—was only the fourth championship in over thirty years.

The record books showed that in season 1904–5 Celtic and Rangers shared the championship, then the Parkhead club went on to win five straight victories in the race for the League flag. And moving slightly to more modern times, Rangers had notched five victories between 1928 and 1933.

I respect the achievements of the giants of these teams—the clubs dominated by Willie Maley and Bill Struth—in relation to the football of their day.

But it has as much relevance to the crowded, pressure-packed fixture list of our era as a Model-T car has to a sleek saloon of the seventies.

The pre-war managers had no League Cup to contend with, in fact the pre-1955 managers had no European competitions to even bother about.

A trip to Aberdeen was the farthest any team could hope to travel for a competitive match, and if there was a Continental trip it was only a close-season tour.

I would not diminish the praise for any team who wins a modern League championship. Football in the sixties, and now into the seventies, is making its own records. They are new records—they have to be because it is such a changing soccer world.

And the record that Celtic have forged, of five straight wins, will stand out as one of the proudest beacons whenever football fans turn to consult their history books.

When, yet again, it was all wrapped up and another flag unfurling ceremony was scheduled, Jock Stein told me: 'I never really had any doubts about the championship. For I knew that if we could keep in touch with the leaders at the New Year then we would go on to win.

'There were two important fixtures out of the thirty-four for they showed the value of getting on with games.

'One was against Dundee United in December at Parkhead, and Partick Thistle at Firhill in February.

'The weather was not good for either of them. We might have tried to get them put off and waited until the end of the season.

'If we had done that, I shudder to think of the mix-up with fixtures we would have been in, just when we wanted to be free of any worries.'

The sight that struck fear into many teams last season . . . as that busy little forward Lou Macari buzzes in on goal. The opponent trying to catch him this time is Ayr United left-back John Murphy

It was a season also where the power of the Parkhead first team pool was never shown to better advantage, as youngsters David Hay—the best discovery of the season—and Louis Macari were brought in to take the place of stars such as Steve Chalmers and John Clark, who missed almost half a year because of injuries.

There was another lengthy absence for Bobby Lennox, injured for three months, Willie Wallace, suspended for a month, and Bobby Murdoch, out for another month when he was sent on a slimming cure.

These were all triumphantly overcome, and the flag was settled for Parkhead a month before the end of the season.

How much had that to do with the astonishing collapse of Rangers, who in February were only waiting for a Celtic slip to pounce into top place . . . yet, by the end of the season, had given away points as if they were Green Shield stamps?

The Celtic boss thought it affected his team also, for he reasoned: 'When Rangers' challenge went, it took a mental edge off my side. Maybe the strain had gone a bit, but the push we got from having to keep an eye in every game on the team who were second disappeared, and perhaps it made them a bit too casual.'

No bands play for a League championship win. It stretches over such a long period it almost seems strange when the campaign is over, for it is something everyone has lived with from August to April.

Yet it is only when you examine the cuttings, which seem so recent yet are already fading, that you realise just how much goes into a championship.

Perhaps the best summing-up of any team who wins the League championship came from Willie Waddell. Not long after he had left his job in journalism to take over at Ibrox, he told me of his aims: 'Cups are fine. We all want to win them. But the League championship is the real test of the character of a team.'

So come back with me to August 1969, to the day the flag for the fourth League championship victory was unfurled . . . and the campaign for the fifth started.

It was against St. Johnstone, the shock team of the start of the season, who had been the highest scorers of the League Cup qualifiers.

The temperature soared to seventy degrees, and so did the excitement as Saints twice took the lead, although Steve Chalmers and then Harry Hood equalised.

80

He's about to take a tumble, but it's well worth it for Harry Hood, *left,* as he slots the ball past Rangers defence for Celtic's goal in their League Cup match at Ibrox

The team went on to pick up full points in traditionally a tough away fixture at Kilmarnock the following Wednesday, with a fine 4–2 victory, the goals were split between Willie Wallace, two, and Bobby Lennox, two.

But no one could have been prepared for the flop which followed against Dunfermline the following Saturday at East End Park.

They were beaten 2–1—and had the worst first-half I could recall from a Celtic side when they lost two goals. Just to complete their misery, centre-forward Willie Wallace was sent off in a thirteenth-minute clash with Willie Renton of Dunfermline. He was the first Celtic player to be sent off in two seasons.

Tommy Gemmell got a second-half goal, but it must have been only a slight consolation for Celtic fans when George Farm, the Dunfermline manager said afterwards: 'We are on top of the world after this result. You really have to go some to beat Celtic.'

There was an even bigger shock to come the next week when they lost by 2–0 to Hibs on their own Parkhead—just before the European Cup match against Basle in Switzerland. And the champions, with only one victory from four League games, were sitting in a very unaccustomed and unhappy eleventh place in the League.

Yet, after all that, and a o–o draw against Basle, they crashed back to one of their finest results of the season, a 1–o victory against Rangers at Ibrox.

Ibrox had been a hoodoo ground in League games; it was their first victory there for eleven years, and the winning goal from Harry Hood was the first in a championship clash at Ibrox since 1967.

A pity it was marred by a second-half ordering-off of right-back Jim Craig, and bookings for Davie Hay, and Sandy Jardine of Rangers.

September ended a little better with a 2–1 victory against Clyde at Shawfield, and Bobby Lennox grabbed both goals.

They really stepped up the pace at the start of October with a 7–1 crushing of Raith Rovers at Parkhead where the scoring hit-parade was split between Jimmy Johnstone, two, Bobby Lennox, two, Willie Wallace, Tom Callaghan and John Hughes.

It was also the first-team début for young Kenny Dalgliesh at right-half, one of the babes given a glimpse of life in the first team last season.

A tough 2–o away victory at Airdrie followed, the scorers were Chalmers and Wallace. But it was more memorable as it was Ronnie Simpson's thirty-ninth birthday and he captained the side because Billy McNeill was ill. And the crowd sang 'Happy Birthday'.

There was another valuable away win at Pittodrie—even more praiseworthy in view of the Cup Final result—with a 3–2 victory at Aberdeen, and the goals came from Bobby Murdoch, Jimmy Johnstone, and a rare score which was the winner from Jim Brogan.

I saw Murdoch touch one of his season's peaks in an exciting 4–2 victory against Ayr United at Somerset Park when he scored the last two goals, and Jimmy Johnstone got the first two.

Then came one of the season's most jarring results, a 2–o defeat by Hearts at Parkhead just before the European Cup victory against Benfica.

Yet with a narrow 2–1 victory, thanks to Harry Hood and Tommy Gemmell, against Motherwell at Fir Park the following week—and only a last-minute goal-line clearance by Jim Craig saved a draw—Celtic really started the march to the championship. It was to be four months before they lost another game, and only one point was dropped in that time . . . wonderful proof that their own consistency wore down every other championship challenger.

They survived the effects of the defeat in Lisbon from Benfica to win 3–0 at Morton, with Macari, Hood and Wallace getting the goals.

Then it was St. Mirren's turn in a postponed match and little Macari was fast establishing himself as a member of the first-team pool with both goals in a 2–0 victory. A new 'keeper was introduced also in this match, Evan Williams.

Ole! This Ayr United defender appeals for a bye kick as inside-right Willie Wallace looks on in the league match at Parkhead

They followed that up with a 1–0 penalty victory against
Dundee . . . the spot-kick was scored by Tommy Gemmell
although the Dens Park side disputed it.

But there was another vital away victory, a 4–1 crushing of
St. Johnstone at Perth as they reached the half-way stage,
and the goals came from Willie Wallace, two, Hood and
Gemmell.

And then came the mid-week match that rocketed them
back to the number one spot in the League table, a position
they were never to lose again for the rest of the season.

It was a 7–2 victory against Dundee United at Parkhead.
The scorers were Wallace, two, Auld, Hood, Gemmell (penalty),
Hughes, Murdoch.

But really the night belonged to Jimmy Johnstone, with
one of his most fantastic displays, when he shows such form he
seems to be reaching out and taking the title of the greatest
winger in Europe.

There was no let-up after that. A 3–1 victory against Kilmarnock, unfortunately remembered for a tragic leg break to
Killie veteran Frank Beattie.

The goals came from Gemmell (penalty), and two from John
Hughes.

It was Christmas, but Celtic pushed on with another scoring
bonanza, an 8–1 victory against Partick Thistle and a hat-trick
for John Hughes, two for Wallace, and the rest from Auld,
McNeill and Campbell, own goal.

Clyde at Shawfield were next, on New Year's Day, and Celtic
had to work for a 2–0 victory with goals from Hughes and Macari.

Then came the old pals 'Old Firm' match, a 0–0 draw
between Celtic and Rangers on a frozen Parkhead, but fortunately free from terracing trouble.

After that came the match which perhaps was the real
turning point for the championship, a 2–1 victory against Hibs
at Easter Road.

Rangers trailed only two slim points behind Celtic, who
were soon to be occupied with European Cup and Scottish
Cup matches.

A slip-up here could have been disastrous, and it seemed
as if one point would go, for although Billy McNeill scored
in the first half, Hibs had equalised; then, with only four
minutes, a shot from John Hughes trundled off a defender
for the winner.

It was all go after that! A 3–1 victory for revenge against
Dunfermline . . . the scorers were Wallace, Macari and Lennox,

and their second victory against the Fife club in two weeks to follow up their Scottish Cup win.

Then a 5–1 trouncing for Partick Thistle, on frozen Firhill, but Tommy Gemmell, with two penalties, Johnstone, Hood and Macari, all scored.

Raith Rovers, Thistle's partner in relegation trouble, were beaten 2–0 at Kirkcaldy in a mid-week fixture after the Scottish Cup victory against Rangers, the scorers were both defenders, McNeill and Gemmell.

Salute to the champions . . . the St. Mirren team applaud John Hughes, the last man out of the Celtic line-up as they run on to Love Street for the final league game

Then Airdrie were beaten 4–2 at Parkhead, the men who scored were Johnstone, two, Lennox, Wallace. But the really significant result that day came from Easter Road where Hibs drew 1–1 with Rangers . . . and the points lead magically stretched to three, the first break in the two-point difference between the sides for over fourteen weeks.

Billy McNeill scored his first-ever double with both goals in a 2–0 victory against Dundee United at Tannadice, then there was a 4–0 victory against Morton, the goals came from Ferguson, own goal, Auld, Macari and Lennox.

Rangers dropped another shock two points that week in March, when they were beaten 2–1 by Raith Rovers, soon to be relegated, at Kircaldy, and the battle was almost over.

There was a 3–0 victory against Ayr United, two goals from Wallace and the other from Lennox, and they were set to clinch the championship against Aberdeen at Parkhead.

It would have been the first of the five to have been won in front of their own fans, the previous victories had been at Motherwell, Ibrox, Dunfermline and Rugby Park.

There were even TV cameras in the dressing-room to record the champagne popping. But the script went wrong, for Aberdeen won 2–1 and not even a last-minute Tommy Gemmell free-kick could save Celtic. It was a result which was to have significant repercussions.

However, the uncorking of the champagne was only delayed three days, for although Gemmell missed a penalty against Hearts at Tynecastle, they drew 0–0 to take the point they needed.

After the great victory at Leeds they sped to a 6–1 crushing of Motherwell, with a welcome hat-trick for Bobby Lennox, a penalty from Wallace and the other two from Johnstone and Murdoch.

And, as Rangers tumbled yet again on the last day of the season with a 1–0 defeat from Morton, Celtic wrapped it all up with a 3–2 victory against St. Mirren at Love Street, when the scorers were Harry Hood, Victor Davidson and Tom Callaghan.

When they had clinched the title that day at Tynecastle, a reporter asked Jock Stein . . . 'Is it true you order League flags wholesale?' The big man just smiled, he knew they do not come as easily as that, despite that fantastic twelve-point lead.

86

JIM BROGAN

The Trouble With 'Old Firm' Games

Flashpoint . . . as Bobby Lennox and Rangers 'keeper Gerry Neef
clash in the Ibrox side's penalty area during the 'Old Firm' Cup match

THE crowd's roars soared to a crescendo as Celtic and Rangers milled about in a pushing, shoving mass of sweat-stained bodies in the middle of the penalty area while, in the centre of the action, the giant figure of referee Tom Wharton attempted to separate the two teams.

It was 21 February 1970, the third round Scottish Cup match between Celtic and Rangers at Parkhead. The score-line was 3-1 in favour of Celtic . . . a fact which almost got obscured in the post-mortems after the match which included a special meeting of Glasgow magistrates and all the players of both teams appearing before the S.F.A. officials at Park Gardens.

I was one of the players involved in that second-half incident, so let me give you my version of the chain of events . . .

The game was locked at 1-1, when Rangers attacked down the left-wing. As our 'keeper Evan Williams dived to smother the ball on the ground, the Ibrox inside-left, Alex McDonald, came charging in as the goalkeeper lay on the ground.

I must be honest about it. I thought at the time, and I still have the same opinion, that McDonald's action in following up was dangerous and Williams could have been seriously injured.

I was standing behind the 'keeper, and I immediately rushed at McDonald to push him away. Before you could snap your fingers the penalty area seemed to be more packed than the terracing.

When referee Wharton finally got it all calmed down, he called the Rangers player over and ordered him off the field. Some commentators thought I should have gone with him.

Perhaps on reflection I was fortunate not to have been cautioned, but it is very difficult not to act when you think a team-mate is going to be injured.

Players do not go out deliberately to have a go at one another in these 'Old Firm' matches. I am convinced of that.

But we get caught up in the tenseness of the occasion; so much is at stake perhaps it pushes players beyond the limits of discipline they would observe in any other match.

I would like to hope that the meeting we all attended at the S.F.A. will bring about a solution, but it would be wishful thinking to pretend it can be the complete answer.

It is not just the players who are responsible. These games have a mixture of ingredients which combine to make them a powder-keg, and it only needs a light to explode it.

For a start, they are derby games—two local teams opposed to one another—and that can cause bother not just in Glasgow.

Flashpoint . . . as Rangers centre Colin Stein 'congratulates' Jim
Craig after an own goal from the Celtic right-back had put the
Ibrox side ahead in the Cup clash at Parkhead

Look at the rivalry which exists in Edinburgh when Hearts
and Hibs clash, or Tyneside when it's Newcastle and Sunder-
land, or Merseyside between Liverpool and Everton.

Celtic fans want to see their team win . . . Rangers supporters
are just as keen it should be their side who finish the victors.

Put it all in a great big melting-pot and add the one ingredient
peculiar to the fixture, religious bigotry, and you have a recipe
for trouble.

Maybe I should say 'so-called religious warfare' between the
fans. Perhaps it is only an excuse, maybe there would still be

bother if it were absent, but it is there and it is a subject which is too often hushed up.

I am sorry to say I think Rangers are the worst offenders with their policy of not signing Catholics for their team.

Aside from any other considerations it is a policy which must hurt them in a football sense, for it cuts off so many promising boys from signing for them.

The Ibrox officials have sometimes said that it would be unfair to ask a Catholic boy to play for Rangers, the reaction from the fans if he did not play well would make life too hard.

But a start has to be made sometime. I would not have been afraid to have played for Rangers—I still would not—and I am sure there must be other players who hold the same views.

I am not a worrier, but every player betrays the tension which he feels before an 'Old Firm' game.

I talk a lot before a game, but I know I talk a lot more before an 'Old Firm' game. Strangely enough, once I get on the field I enjoy·playing in the matches, although I know many players in both teams dislike the matches intensely.

Of course, I talk a lot during any game. It is a habit of mine, and I am happy to say my team-mates do not seem to mind. Why should I blether away during a match? Well, in some of our games, the ordinary League matches, some of the team occasionally get too complacent. It's sometimes difficult when we are playing perhaps one of the Continent's top teams to adjust to a League game at home.

Yet they are all important, and we have to treat them that way. I might shout at one of my colleagues, but equally they have the right to shout back, and after the match there are no hard feelings.

After all, we have the same objective . . . a winning Celtic team.

But I know my voice is not the element of my game that causes criticism, it is my reputation as a tackler.

I consider I am a hard tackler, and I make no apologies for it. My job is basically defensive, but I must admit I find slightly unsettling the allegations that my tackling is over-keen.

I play hard, but I try to play the ball at all times. And, although my main role is as sweeper, I am allowed to go up the park sometimes, so I don't think it's all destructive, my work during the game.

I've no desire to play centre-forward. But there are occasions when I think I can take part in the play when it is in our opponents' half of the field.

Eye on the ball for guidance, arms outstretched for balance . . . and
Jim Brogan brings the fierce determination to a clearance in a
practice match which is his trademark during a game

I believe all players today must strive to be real professionals, the rewards in football are so great now.

But, perhaps almost as important, the image of a footballer has improved in the years since I have been a senior player.

People no longer look down on footballers as having their brains only in their feet. Many factors have achieved this, but the three football events which helped most of all were England's World Cup victory in 1966, Celtic in the European Cup the following year, and Manchester United in 1968.

These three victories, coming one after the other, gave people who perhaps never thought about football, a new impression of the game.

As far as Scottish football is concerned, one vital difference for the top clubs is that all depend now entirely on full-time players in their first-team pools.

I have heard all the arguments for and against full-time football, and I know the part-timers can often match a full-time team for one match, or even keep up in a respectable position for one season.

But I speak from experience on both sides of the fence, and I say without hesitation that, at the level Celtic operate, it would be impossible to be anything else other than a full-time player.

When I joined Celtic in 1963 from the junior side, St. Rochs —the same team as Jimmy McGrory came from—I was a part-timer.

I was an apprentice chartered accountant during the day, I then went to Parkhead twice a week for my training sessions, and back home to continue my studies.

I am not afraid to admit it was a shattering schedule, although I was lucky enough to make my break-through into the first team. And I even played about a dozen games in the same side as my brother Frank, before he was transferred to Ipswich.

However, when Mr. Stein became the manager he made it very clear that he wanted only full-time players in his first team. The era of working during the day, training at night, and then hoping to make a first-team place was over.

I waited almost another two years before I took the decision to go full-time. It was in the November following the European Cup victory against Inter-Milan in Lisbon . . . a campaign that I had played little or no part in.

I. realised then that the club was rising so fast in stature that if I wanted to be a really successful member of it, I had to devote my full attention to it.

Since then I have been more or less regular in the first team, so naturally it is a decision I have never regretted.

However, recently I have been combining both worlds a bit more. Most players look to the future by trying to build up a business while they are still involved in football.

I am no exception, my interest is in a garage, and I manage to split up my day between it and football.

My routine starts with a quick look in at the garage in the morning on my way to training to attend to any mail. Then after the morning training I go back and work in the garage during the afternoon.

I must emphasise that football comes first. There is no question of us skipping a training session, or not going away with the team because of our business interests, and that applies to all the lads who have a business.

But I am grateful for the garage, and I also have plans for other interests. I find it is a safety valve for me. While football is never really out of mind—the customers like to talk about it—I think I would find it a bit of a drag if I had nothing to occupy my time after training.

Mind you, in the hectic wind-up to the season last spring, everyone's mind was concentrated completely on football.

We spent a lot of the time down at our hide-outs on the Ayrshire coast, either at Seamill or at Troon. Most of our wives have young families, and naturally they are not all that happy about being left on their own.

But they realise it is all for the good of the team. For one thing we can get away from callers asking for tickets, and we can really discuss tactics for the various games.

I consider I am very lucky to have been around Parkhead at a time when the club has known so much success.

Some players, like my brother Frank, were unlucky enough to have been transferred just before the great revival. I think he's still a bit disappointed he missed out on it.

However, perhaps it worked out well for me that way. Two brothers playing in the same team can cause a few problems for each other. When I went to Celtic at first, I was better known as Frank Brogan's brother.

Now I am glad to say I think I have made it on my own, and that's something I know I could not have done if I had stayed part-time.

I wish I could give some advice to any boy who might be in the same position as myself, but it is difficult to make hard and fast rules.

The lad must decide how much time he aims to give his studies, and how much he really wants to be a professional footballer. But he must remember that in the high stakes of present-day soccer, there can be really no half-way house.

I consider myself fortunate. I have one set of exams to complete before I would qualify to be a chartered accountant. It would need two or three months' intensive study to prepare for these examinations, and I still hope to sit them one day.

But, as you can imagine, I'm kept pretty busy with football just now . . . and I hope it stays that way for a long time to come!

Flashpoint . . . as referee Tom Wharton separates the rival players after a punch-up in the Rangers penalty area, during that controversial cup-tie

Champions of Britain

IT WAS the night the Hampden roar was born again, and it seemed it would never fade as it went on, and on and on . . . For it was the night a bright new chapter, a very special chapter, was written into Scottish football history as Celtic swept to triumph in the European Cup semi-final against Leeds United.

It was a scene which seared itself indelibly into the memory of every watching fan, and there were 135,000 packed into Hampden's antiquated stands and terraces that night.

I have reported football matches in three continents, I have been awed by hysterical South American crowds, fanatical Italians, the disciplined chants of the Germans.

But I have never seen, nor heard, anything in fan fervour to equal that April night at Hampden . . . Who says the Scots are a dour, unemotional race?

The noise from the crowd that night, as if it was trapped by the Hampden stands, rushed upwards like a whirlpool of sound as it soared past the heights of the press-box to assault the ear-drums.

And, down below, on the neatly manicured turf—another triumph compared to the shocking state of Britain's other giant stadium, Wembley—were the men who had sparked it all off.

The mask had slipped from Jock Stein. He was on the field hugging his players, running in a frenzy from one to another, and really his congratulations were for every fan sandwiched into that stadium.

Then his players set off on a weird and wonderful lap of honour. Some had only their shorts on, some had their boots off, some were clutching as prizes the jerseys of the team they had vanquished as they ran around the pitch with their arms held high like Roman gladiators, and trailed by a panting posse of photographers.

It was the night Glasgow belonged to Celtic, more than any other occasion in the club's history . . . yes, even more than the European Cup Final victory of 1967.

For the majority of fans had only been able to share the Lisbon glory by sitting in front of a television set . . . Hampden was an occasion when they shared the joy of every dazzling move, the agony when anything went wrong.

And, towering above it all, was the age-old formula to unite any Scots, the marvellous realisation that they had triumphed over the English. This was Scottish nationalism expressing itself. Not with guns, not even at the ballot box . . . but in pride of a football team.

There had never been a clash between the Scottish and English champions in the European Cup before—it had an added spice as soccer's Battle of Britain—I reckon more words were spilled about it than any other match.

So let's flash back to the twenty-six-day life of this tie, from the draw in Rome which gave it birth, to the final moment when victorious Celtic disappeared up the Hampden tunnel.

A few weeks before the semi-final, when both still had their quarter-final ties to fight, I had spoken to Leeds manager Don Revie and Jock Stein in a joint interview about the possibility of a clean sweep of all the trophies, both were poised in a position to win the European Cup, their respective F.A. Cups and League championships.

Neither were eventually to achieve it, although Revie summed up how hard it would be when he first used to me a phrase he was to repeat over and over again . . . 'If we do succeed, then it will be the eighth wonder of the world.'

After the draw the soccer spy business started, and it was a game played in deadly earnest. Leeds have a system where manager Revie rarely looks at opposing teams, instead he sends his famed spy double-team of assistant manager Maurice Lindlay and chief coach Syd Owen.

The Leeds pair are relied on completely by Revie for their judgements on any opposing team. They even give stars on a player's courage, all part of a thirty-two page dossier they filed on Celtic.

Yet I believe Celtic got an immediate advantage. Stein, wiliest of all tacticians, warned that he would switch his team around, and he did just that to such an extent that one Leeds official privately admitted they were baffled.

For Leeds there could be no luxury of concealment. They were committed to an F.A. Cup semi-final against Manchester United which was to stretch to 300 minutes of football, made up of the first match, the replay plus extra time, and eventually a third match.

It took them from Hillsbrough in Sheffield, to Villa Park in Birmingham, and finally to Burnden Park, Bolton, and only one goal—scored by Leeds skipper Billy Bremner—in the third game, broke the deadlock.

And in the stands, watching the games at Birmingham and Bolton, was Jock Stein, weighing up, as only he can, the strengths and weaknesses of Leeds.

So they headed for the first leg at Elland Road, but not before Leeds sensationally rocked English soccer, for the week before they met Celtic their diary consisted of these two F.A. Cup semi-final replays, and a League match with Southampton at home.

Some of the first team were rested for the League game, they were beaten 3–1 in a shock result, and their chances of one major prize, the English First Division championship, virtually disappeared.

But that was only a tremor compared to the match they had

Two to one, as Leeds United left-back Terry Cooper and 'keeper Garry Sprake get into a tangle to take the ball away from Jimmy Johnstone, one of the few times they managed it

to play at Derby two days later, when the entire first-team squad were left out and Leeds lost 4–1 amid a storm of controversy.

So Leeds lost the championship, but Celtic went to Elland Road as champions. They had slipped up against Aberdeen the week before, however they clinched it against Hearts.

As Celtic's train was rolling south to their pre-match headquarters in Harrogate, Don Revie was giving a press conference at Elland Road.

Some of the English critics who so freely tipped a Leeds win should perhaps have listened more carefully to Revie's words. They thought it would be easy . . . he did not!

He said: 'As far as I am concerned Celtic are as great as any of the great teams from Europe we have played in the last five seasons.' And he praised especially Jimmy Johnstone: 'His skills are on a par with those of Best. He is every bit as good a player.

'We must win at Elland Road. A draw is no use to us. We must either get a 1–0 or a 2–0 victory at Elland Road.'

And later that day Jock Stein was saying the same thing about Johnstone to his own players at a secret tactics talk.

He gathered them all around the portable tactics board he had taken with him, lifted off the number seven marker, held it up, and declared: 'This is the player who can win it for us.'

Stein's first idea had been to play Johnstone at centre against Leeds, to let him buzz round and try to destroy Jack Charlton.

But a look at Leeds had convinced him that pressure on their left flank, reckoned to be their strongest defensively, could pay off.

The teams were:

Leeds: Sprake, Reaney, Cooper; Bremner, Charlton, Madeley; Lorimer, Clarke, Jones, Giles, Gray.

Celtic: Williams, Hay, Gemmell; Murdoch, McNeill, Brogan; Johnstone, Connelly, Wallace, Lennox, Auld.

Officially Celtic received only 6,000 tickets for the game, but many more fans had obviously obtained one of these precious slips of cardboard, for there was just as full-throated a roar for the Scots when they appeared as there had been for the Yorkshire side.

But it was nothing to the noise made only forty seconds after the kick-off when Celtic snatched the lead, the injection of confidence to one side and numbing despair to the other team which every manager wants, and can really only hope will happen.

98

A ground-level view as John Hughes sprawls on to the Hampden turf after his equaliser, and the stunned Leeds defence can only stand and stare

The ball went down the left inside Celtic's half of the pitch. It was played back down the field, and Leeds seemed mesmerised as George Connelly—how he fooled those of us who imagined he would be in a defensive role!—swooped on the ball to shoot it off left-back Cooper's legs, and it trundled away from Sprake and over the line.

Celtic then went on to add the gloss and soccer style to that goal with a memorable display. Remember this was Elland Road, the ground reckoned by every English First Division club to be the most difficult to even snatch a draw.

Behind me in the stand one truculent Yorkshire fan could only gasp as he watched Celtic outplay his side: 'They put seventeen players on for the warm-up, I don't think they've taken any of them off.'

Leeds were finding it difficult to even get to the ball as Celtic tightened their grip on the game, and it was topped-off by one player—the man Jock Stein wanted to tear Leeds apart—Jimmy Johnstone.

My Yorkshire friend lost his dourness to admit: 'They say he's as good as Best . . . no he's not, he's better.'

The goal that wrapped it all up . . . as Bobby Murdoch (*extreme left*) beats off a challenge from Johnny Giles to shoot home Celtic's second goal at Hampden

One move will always stand out in my mind, a jewel as near perfect as can be worked on a football field: a sweeping dash down the right by David Hay, Johnstone, and ending in a shot fired in by Bobby Murdoch, which just cleared the bar.

So at half time the Celtic banners waved with joy, but no wonder Don Revie feels he does not get the support from Leeds to which his team are entitled. They rarely rose above the sort of backing I would expect to hear at an ordinary League game.

The game had only ticked fifty seconds into the second half when Connelly had belted the ball into the back of the net again. This time it was disallowed for off-side against Johnstone, although it could have been only by a millimetre.

Still, the linesman had flagged as soon as the ball broke to Johnstone and before he had passed to Connelly.

Leeds edged into the game after that, you could hardly discount a team of their class, but they persisted in sticking to tactics of high crosses into the Celtic goal, which were efficiently disposed of by Billy McNeill and his defensive mates.

It was a tactic which was useless in Europe ten years ago,

I must admit I was surprised to see Leeds—the so-modern side—
stick rigidly to it.

There was one anxious moment when every Scottish heart
stopped as Eddie Gray crashed a shot off the bar, but there was
rarely much more to seriously disturb the Scots' composure.

Celtic were still keen to get a second goal, so anxious that
when 'keeper Evan Williams signalled he was injured as his
team waited to take a corner at the other end, an angry Jock
Stein himself ran on to the park for a quick inspection, to tell
his goalkeeper to get on with the game.

Leeds had to take off Billy Bremner, suffering from con-
cussion, and for the last twenty minutes Celtic substituted
John Hughes for George Connelly, whose tall frame had been
so effective in winning the battle of the mid-field.

And so it finished with Celtic still guarding carefully that
one-goal lead, and in fact the only success of Leeds was after
the game when they won the toss to decide that if a play-off
was needed, it would be at Sheffield Wednesday's ground,
Hillsbrough.

And it was nice to record that a Leeds police spokesman—after all the fuss about shutting shops and pubs—described the 10,000 Celtic fans' behaviour as 'exemplary'.

Johnstone and David Hay, the right-back who only a year previously had been in the obscurity of the reserves, were the talk of England.

The little right-winger was valued by some experts at a massive £250,000.

Leeds' misery that week was complete when right-back Paul Reaney suffered a broken leg the day after the European Cup game in a match at West Ham.

There was a fortnight between the two ties, but nobody could say it was a fortnight's rest. The League programme ground on, and the Saturday before Hampden both teams had F.A. Cup finals.

For Leeds, who had been given almost a week off, there was a morale-boosting match at Wembley when, even although it went to extra time, they did everything but defeat Chelsea, and Eddie Gray was named 'Man of the Match'.

For Celtic there was a morale-jolting 3–1 defeat from Aberdeen in the Scottish Cup Final at Hampden. And, perhaps just as important, an ankle injury to Billy McNeill, which meant a desperate race against time to get him fit for the game.

How much had Leeds' fierce programme before the first Celtic match contributed to their defeat at Elland Road? You argued from whatever side you supported, but there could be no excuses for Hampden.

Revie himself made that clear when he said: 'We have been told that no team who are a goal down at home in a European Cup semi-final have ever reached the final of the tournament. But we won't let that worry us because we are history-makers, we are record-breakers . . . and if ever a record can go, this one can.'

McNeill was officially declared fit only hours before the kick-off—physiotherapist Bob Rooney had worked on him until 1 a.m. the morning of the match—but there was a pre-match blow to Celtic when Willie Wallace was suddenly hit by a foot injury and had to withdraw.

But Rooney's work, rightly praised by Jock Stein, had been invaluable . . . it was by his efforts that the centre-half was able to play.

The team was:

Celtic: Williams, Hay, Gemmell; Murdoch, McNeill, Brogan; Johnstone, Connelly, Hughes, Auld and Lennox.

Leeds had the iron man of English football, Norman Hunter, back at left-half in a team which read: Sprake; Madeley, Cooper; Bremner, Charlton, Hunter; Lorimer, Clarke, Jones, Giles, Gray.

What a reception Celtic got at the start! Thousands crammed around the top of the Hampden terracings, some of them hardly able to see, but still ready to shout on the Scots.

There were early escapes for Leeds, and when Sprake failed to cut out a Murdoch shot he got a blasting from Charlton. Then, suddenly, the goal lead that Celtic had clung on to since the first minute of Elland Road, and for 15 minutes of Hampden, had disappeared.

Bertie Auld failed to cut out the ball going to Billy Bremner, and from just inside his own half the little Leeds skipper sped on to unleash a shot which sped venomously towards goal, helped at the last moment by a swerve which—as if it had been a rocket programmed by a computer—blasted it into the net.

This, more than any other moment of the match, was the supreme test of Celtic's character. They must have sneaked a thought about the previous Saturday at Hampden; would they crack again?

Hampden's greatest moment of the season . . . as Celtic, led by skipper Billy McNeill, run that never-to-be-forgotten lap of honour after their victory against Leeds

For Leeds, it was the tactical pay-off they had wanted. The place in the final seemed comfortably close again.

Yet, spurred on by a superb Bertie Auld in mid-field, Celtic showed just why they deserved to be going to Milan.

I must admit I expected that goal to revive Leeds, but confidence never really rippled through the team. Instead, Paul Madeley had to desperately hook a Bobby Lennox shot off the line, and slowly it dawned on the crowd that it was Celtic who were back in their old familiar attacking routine.

Two minutes after half time the pay-off they had worked so hard to achieve arrived. David Hay forced Hunter to concede a corner on the right, the right-back took a short kick to Auld who whipped it over for John Hughes to sprawl himself on to the Hampden turf to head the ball past Sprake.

They took so long to congratulate each other that even Jock Stein dashed out of his dug-out to wave them to get on with the game.

Then Sprake, who had been nervy right through the match, was injured when he dived at the feet of Hughes, and there was the sad sight of him being take off lying on a stretcher.

Now was Celtic's chance and, like the champions they are, they advanced for the kill. Remember there was the agonising thought that if Leeds had scored again, and the game had finished 2–2, the English side would have won, with their away goals counting double.

But substitute 'keeper David Harvey was allowed one goal-kick at the ball before he touched it again, as he lifted it from the back of his own net.

Again another magical move down the right between John-stone and Murdoch, and the right-half—in one move he seemed to shrug aside all the form problems which had plagued him during the season—as he lashed the ball low through the Leeds defence and into the net.

It was only 51 minutes, but it was all over. Leeds brought on Mick Bates for Lorimer, switched Bremner to centre in a desperate gamble to get back into the game. But, amazingly, their only real shot in anger had been that goal from their captain.

It had been a complete and overwhelming triumph. And as the watches on every waiting fan inched around to full time, a massive chant of 'Jock Stein, Jock Stein' swept round and round Hampden, a tribute to the man who had master-minded Celtic's triumph.

The final whistle from the so-efficient German referee,

Gerhard Schulenberg, was the signal for those wonderful scenes of triumph. An English journalist sitting near me said wistfully: 'They've got everything but the Cup down there.'

And why not? It was the first time a Scottish team had beaten Leeds in five attempts in a European competition, and the pride of England had lost the tag they had been given of 'Europe's best' . . . the label had been well and truly ripped off by Celtic's brilliance.

When Celtic won the European Cup in 1967, there had been some of soccer's cynics who had contemptuously dismissed it as a bad year, although how there can be such a thing in the champions Cup, I have never been able to work out.

No one could say it was a bad year this time. The final overpowering triumph was that they won away from home, and at home. Every team dreams about doing it to Leeds, the measure of Celtic's achievement is that few succeed.

The one that got away . . . Leeds manager Don Revie holds the £1,000 manager of the year award, as Jock Stein—the man Revie said should have won it—looks on

The Scottish Cup Campaign

The long arm of Aberdeen 'keeper Bobby Clark gets a little longer
as a hidden hand gives his jersey a tug during a goalmouth
incident in the Cup Final

THE final whistle blew, the crowd roared its acclamation from
the terracing, the winners hurled themselves into little ecstatic
groups all over the pitch.

It was the traditional end-of-the-match scenes at a Cup Final,
but this time for Celtic it was tinged with disappointment.

They had to endure the unfamiliar role of runners-up and

stand back to watch Aberdeen march up to collect the Scottish Cup . . . and the Parkhead dream of a clean sweep of all the trophies, a repeat of 1967, was shattered.

It had seemed such a pre-match certainty, the bookmakers had stretched the odds against Aberdeen taking the Cup north for the first time in 23 years to a fantastic 6 to 1 against.

The evidence of the League game two weeks before when Aberdeen had beaten Celtic in a shock 2–1 victory at Parkhead was forgotten . . . it was felt that the champions were looking over their shoulders at the forthcoming European Cup first leg against Leeds.

Maybe they were still looking over their shoulders at the second leg against Leeds when the Cup Final came around.

Jock Stein, to his credit, had stated both on TV and in the Press before the match that he felt it would not be a bad thing for Scottish football generally if Aberdeen won the Cup . . . but they would have to fight to take it off Celtic.

Yet strangely, the Scottish Cup—once the main trophy for which Celtic were noted for winning—was the only domestic honour the team had failed to clinch in two successive seasons since Stein moved to Parkhead.

They had lifted it in 1965, the very first trophy of the successful Stein-Celtic partnership when they beat Dunfermline, they lost to Rangers in a Cup Final replay the following season, beat Aberdeen in 1967, lost to Dunfermline in 1968 and beat Rangers in 1969.

There was to be no repeat victory in 1970, partly due to the fact that Celtic were never allowed by Aberdeen to put on the sort of soccer style which has become their big-game trademark.

But it would also be wrong to ignore the fact that three controversial decisions by the referee, Bobby Davidson, helped to swing the Cup away from Celtic.

The first moment of controversy came in 27 minutes when Mr. Davidson—he was the only Scottish referee picked for the World Cup Finals in Mexico—gave a penalty decision against Celtic.

An innocent cross from right-winger Derek McKay hit Bobby Murdoch, but there seemed to be no deliberate attempt by the Celtic right-half to play the ball, it was far from the goal anyway, away out on the edge of the 18-yard box.

None of the Celtic protests changed the referee's mind, left-back Tommy Gemmell had his name taken for throwing the ball to the referee, and after the fuss had died down Joe Harper scored with the penalty.

The road to the final . . . one of the great moments for Celtic
as Rangers 'keeper Gerry Neef sprawls on the Parkhead turf, and
team-mate Willie Wallace raises his arm to salute the goal from
Jimmy Johnstone (*not in picture*) which pushed the score to 3—1

Then four minutes later there was another storm swirling
around the referee. Aberdeen 'keeper Bobby Clark had been
noticeably edgy with his clearances, especially when he was
challenged by any of the Celtic forwards.

Just as he had done before in the match Bobby Lennox
positioned himself in front of the 'keeper in an eyeball confrontation, and when Clark dropped the ball the little inside-
man swiftly struck to swoop on to the ball and drive it into the
empty net.

But the referee disallowed it, and this time Jimmy Johnstone's name was put in the referee's book for showing dissent
at the decision, his first caution of the season.

However, the most numbing blow, and one where I and
almost every other press-man, disagreed with the referee, came
in 38 minutes when he turned aside Celtic's claims for a
penalty after Lennox had been tumbled by Aberdeen captain
Martin Buchan.

Perhaps the referee could claim that the ball had struck

Murdoch's hand for the Aberdeen penalty, perhaps he could claim that a linesman had flagged to disallow the Lennox goal . . . unfortunately they are not allowed to speak about decisions, but I wonder what the reasons were for that judgement on the disallowed penalty.

A trio of decisions like that can upset any team's composure, yet Celtic—who in their vastly experienced European programme had suffered decisions with which they disagreed—allowed it obviously to ruffle them.

There was still only one goal in it, yet in the second half, despite a barrage of pressure they could not snap the equaliser.

It was Aberdeen who broke away only 10 minutes from time and right-winger McKay—he had been signed by the Dons on a free transfer from Dundee—caught out the stretched Celtic defence with the help of centre Jim Forrest, to score.

Lennox did pull one back for Celtic a minute from time, but just to show that they were worthy Cup-holders, that little man McKay scored a third for Aberdeen right on time.

And although many Celtic supporters left before the end it was to the credit of the vast majority of Parkhead fans that they waited to applaud Aberdeen receive the Cup they deserved to win on their form that day.

It was a pity that Jock Stein's after-match congratulations to Aberdeen were almost buried in the Celtic manager's remarks about his annoyance at the referee's decisions.

Controversy and the Cup were never very far apart in last season's competition, and there was an even bigger storm over the third-round tie between Celtic and Rangers at Parkhead in February.

This was the two teams on a collision course, and it exploded into one of the bitterest brawls I have seen between them.

It was spotlighted on two second half incidents when each 'keeper, first Rangers' Gerry Neef then Celtic's Evan Williams, were injured and the field looked like a bar-room punch-up in a scene from a Western movie.

Both managers, Jock Stein and Willie Waddell, had sensibly tried to calm down the tension in the week before the match, but in the first 10 minutes all their good intentions were swept away.

Celtic almost got the boost any side wants in these games, the vital early goal, when in only four minutes a Tommy Gemmell shot bounced off Neef straight to Lennox, and although Alex McDonald had backtracked to scoop it clear, the Celtic players claimed it was over the line.

The Hampden consolation . . . as Bobby Lennox races on to score
Celtic's goal in the Scottish Cup Final—and the Aberdeen
defence are split—at Hampden

Then two minutes later came a crushing blow, when a cross from Colin Stein was headed by right-back Jim Craig into his own net, and it lit the fuse which was to explode later.

For two Rangers' forwards, Willie Johnston and Colin Stein, raced up to ruffle Craig's hair in congratulations, while Celtic centre, Willie Wallace, took off after Johnstone to exact his own personal retribution.

The busiest man on the park was going to be referee Tom Wharton, but in that turbulent first half only one player was cautioned, John Greig.

Celtic had grabbed the equaliser, a smart shot by Bobby Lennox in 39 minutes, and at half time it was one each.

Four minutes after the restart any hopes that the interval would have cooled the match down were swept aside when there was a major punch-up in the Rangers' penalty area.

Lennox had clashed with Neef, and the referee had to dive in to separate fist-swinging players, and he had to repeat the role yet again in 60 minutes.

This time it was Rangers' inside-left Alex McDonald who raced in on Williams. As the 'keeper crumpled to the ground, Celtic left-half Jim Brogan leapt at the Rangers' player, and another free-for-all started.

It ended with McDonald being sent off by Mr. Wharton and kids spilling over on to the track at the Rangers' end before the trouble was eased.

Some club officials felt later that too much had been made of the violence, yet it was an undeniable fact that the two goal-mouth punch-ups were incidents more likely to be seen in the English First Division than on any Scottish ground.

So it was Celtic's 11 against Rangers' 10, and just when it seemed that the Ibrox side might manage to force a replay, the Parkhead side struck.

And it was a goal worthy of winning any game, a fabulous 30-yard shot from inside-right David Hay, the sort of move which can break any scoring deadlock, and the victory was topped off with a third goal, from Jimmy Johnstone only two minutes later.

It was unfortunate that a Celtic victory—and not just in terms of the 3–1 score-line but in tactics as well—was overwhelmed by the ugly incidents.

For the master-stroke had been Jock Stein's decision to play young David Hay, normally a full-back, in the midfield to blunt the menace of John Greig.

The Rangers' skipper was never allowed to start any of

those powerful rushes which have brought his side so many goals.

The plan was Stein's . . . the man who put it into practice so effectively was the unflinching Hay, who showed that he has those rare twin skills in a footballer, strength and skill.

The recriminations from the game dragged on! Glasgow's magistrates came out with a ridiculous condemnation of the two captains, Billy McNeill of Celtic and Rangers' John Greig, for not trying to restrain their team mates.

Heads who wins? As Aberdeen centre-forward Jim Forrest and Celtic left-back Tommy Gemmell battle for possession during the Scottish Cup Final

Then both teams, their managers and chairmen, were called to a special meeting by the S.F.A. to try to solve an almost insoluble problem.

The S.F.A. at least showed some honesty when they replied to the Glasgow magistrates by stating that they could not be sure they had found any real solution.

It was an unusual Cup draw for Celtic, yet again they played all their ties at home—apart from the semi-final and final—and they were all against top First Division clubs.

Harry Hood snapped the winner only a minute from time against Dunfermline, after the Fife side had scored first and John Hughes had equalised in 80 minutes.

They had a far easier passage in the next round against Dundee United with a 4–0 victory . . . and the scorers were two from John Hughes, Louis Macari and Willie Wallace.

Then came that controversial Rangers' match, and a 2–1 semi-final victory against Dundee when the scorers were Macari and a late winner from Bobby Lennox when the Dens Park 'keeper, Alistair Donaldson, dropped the ball at his feet.

The Cup Final was the first of two Hampden appearances in five days for Celtic. Football allows no side the luxury of picking which trophies they would like to win, but in retrospect, looking at these two Hampden dates—the Scottish Cup Final and the European Cup semi-final against Leeds—I don't believe there's much doubt about which one the team or fans would have chosen!

The Most Vital Match

Taking it easy . . . and the family line-up is Bertie Auld, his
alsatian Cindy, and young Robert junior

IT WAS only a Glasgow Cup fixture, not perhaps the most
glamorous of games in today's star-studded fixture list . . . but,
for me, it was the most important match of last season.

Yes, even more than the League Cup final, the Scottish
Cup final, or any of these wonderful European Cup matches.

Before you think I have suddenly rated the Glasgow Cup
as the most important trophy of them all, maybe I had better
explain.

It was last October, and my first-team appearances had been
few and far between for Celtic as the early months of the season
ticked away.

Then, one morning, the manager Mr. Stein called me into his office after training. He told me that St. Mirren had made an offer for me, and asked me what I thought of a move to Love Street.

I just did not know what to think. I still believed that I could claim a place in Celtic's first team, but there was no denying that a lot of very bright kids were pushing for a top place, and I had a fight on my hands.

The manager said that if I did want to go then he would not stand in my way. But it was such a big decision I obviously could not make it hastily, so I asked for time to think it over.

I was on the point of deciding that the time had come when I would be leaving Celtic, then along came that Glasgow Cup game.

It was against Clyde at Parkhead, and the side was a mixture of the first-team pool, a youngster, Victor Davidson, and our new goalkeeper, Evan Williams.

Clyde scored first, but I snatched the equaliser and we went on to win 4–1. It was a game where I really felt good, everything seemed to go just right.

And by the end of the week I found that my mind had been made up for me, by Mr. Stein. I was back in his office, this time to be told that I would not be leaving Celtic. Can you blame me for thinking that was the best bonus of the season?

I realise, of course, that I can't go on for ever . . . I think some of the youngsters at the park believe I was around when Willie Maley was the manager.

I do not know when I shall finally retire. But, in my heart, I will know when the time to quit comes around. If I cannot put into the game as much as I always have, if I find myself labouring, then I will consider it will be time for me to hang up my boots.

I did not enter for the sprints in the Commonwealth Games last season, but I don't think I am slow over the period which really matters most, the first twenty yards.

I know that when, like me, you get over 21, you expect to slow down a little, but to hear some people talk you would think I needed a jet-propelled wheel-chair to get around a park.

The last few years have been the most marvellous of my career, in fact of any of the lads at Celtic Park. But I do not write off the time before that, far from it.

I know a lot of people in England considered me a flop when I played with Birmingham City. They always seem surprised that I am having any sort of success.

Another medal, but another warning also for Bertie Auld from referee John Paterson after the Celtic winger had belted the ball into the Hampden stand at the end of the League Cup Final against St. Johnstone

I have even heard it on television when a commentator asked the manager about how I have been changed. Fortunately Mr. Stein had the answer: 'He's got a European Cup medal, and that's more than most of the great players in England.'

Well, I am not going to say Sir Alf Ramsey wished I had been born an Englishman when I was at Birmingham . . . but I did not consider myself a flop when I was there.

The fact that some of the English press-men forget is that I did not play with a club which was particularly fashionable. And, just as in Scotland, if you don't play with the really big teams then you don't get rated so highly.

But, let me tell you, not all the players even in the top teams are top stars, and that includes Leeds.

When I came back to Parkhead, just before Mr. Stein, I never felt I was returning as a reject. The Birmingham City manager, it was Joe Mallet then, and the board had let me decide whether or not I should sign again for Celtic.

I was back at Parkhead under different circumstances from when I departed. I realised that the boys I had left when they were fresh-faced teenagers had matured, it could not be long before they exploded into a winning side.

And the spark was lit when Jock Stein followed a month later, for his second spell with the club . . . maybe football is better the second time around.

The switch which really turned out to be effective for me was my first move to inside-forward, a change which was first worked on in the 1966 tour of America.

I had never been an orthodox touch-line winger. I liked to get into the action, for I always felt that out on the wing you had to depend too much on the service of other players.

So it was not such a drastic change, but it did put me alongside Bobby Murdoch in mid-field, and we struck up almost a telepathic understanding of where the other was on the park.

I swear that in the 1967 European Cup Final, even if I had been blindfolded, I would have known where to have found Bobby on that Lisbon park.

The manager's instructions were always that the ball had to go from the back four to the mid-field, Bobby and myself. Only in emergencies was it to be belted up the park.

Strict tactics have a part to play in the modern game, but I reckon an understanding like that between two players can never be forged by any pre-match schemes. Maybe we were luckier than most teams. We have one of the greatest tactical managers in the game, yet our formulas allow for improvisation.

Sometimes the manager's talks last only ten minutes, sometimes they last two hours, yet Mr. Stein can talk away without ever repeating himself.

We don't have these talks before every game. I think he considers that, as the team has matured, so they are able to take more responsibility themselves.

Yet when he does talk he digs up facts as if he was a computer. When he watched Leeds in the two F.A. Cup semi-final replays against Manchester United, he was able to tell us exactly how many times their two link-men, Billy Bremner and Johnny Giles, picked the ball up in the middle of the park.

Just try counting the number of passes one player makes the next time you are at a match, and you will get some idea how difficult it is.

So in the European Cup semi-final he wanted me to make sure Billy Bremner did not get the ball, to cut out the supply to him, and even—although I am not the world's greatest tackler—to try to dispossess him.

And, apart from one lapse, in the second game at Hampden, for which I blame myself, it worked well. But full credit to Bremner . . . that goal he scored was one of the best Hampden has seen for years.

Maybe Jock Stein's secret is that he never asks a player to do a job that is impossible, for he knows that if someone does not have football ability then all the tactics in the world cannot help him.

These so-tense matches against Leeds did not allow me to indulge in a little bit of showmanship. I do not apologise for making the crowd laugh a bit sometimes. The Celtic crowd are the greatest in the world, and I think they like to see a few tricks now and then.

But it sometimes lands me in hot water with the manager. I remember once at Shawfield sitting on the ball. Perhaps he will stand for some of my showmanship, but that particular act was definitely not top of the bill with him.

And, after the game, I was told so in no uncertain manner. Maybe I borrowed a few of the tricks from Charlie Tully, who was still at Parkhead when I joined . . . there I go, giving you more clues about my age again.

I think Charlie was a great player, and would have been a great player in any age. All the talk about comparing past and present football is a lot of hot air as far as I am concerned.

I have been fifteen years in top-class football, and I have seen some fantastic changes since them. But, as I have already said, there is only one yardstick to judge a player—has he ability?

And if a player in the old days showed that, then good luck to him! He would have been a success today, once the training sharpened him up.

As a kid I got myself a bit of a reputation for getting into trouble, ordered off playing for Scotland against Holland, and ordered off after a famous punch-up with Johnny Haynes, then England's number-one name, when I was with Birmingham.

I'm not proud of it all when I look back, but I also feel that it was part of the process of growing up in soccer.

I took a bit of stick from some English writers about a tackle on Leeds centre Mick Jones in the semi-final at Hampden. I don't know if they will believe me, but it was perfectly accidental and happened so simply.

I was looking to push the ball to Billy McNeill in mid-field, but I let it roll slightly too far ahead of me. I stretched to try to send it on to Billy, then big Mick came charging in to tackle and collided with me.

It was as straightforward as that, although to read some comments it seemed as if it was the worst foul in football.

Some of the Leeds players did not like it. They made that pretty clear by what they told me. Maybe we should have switched the subject, and talked about superstitions.

Leeds are supposed to be the most superstitious team in the League, and I go in for a bit of it myself.

My family have always been superstitious, especially my mother. She always said that if you saw a bit of coal in the street you had always to pick it up for luck . . . we had the best fires in Glasgow!

I never walked under ladders as a kid, and I can't get out of the habit to this day. If the team lose when I am wearing a particular suit, it gets put to the back of my wardrobe for a long time.

I would like to chuck it away, but I can't do that . . . my name is Auld, not Onassis. Anyway, I would need to be like George Best and keep a boutique if I really wanted to take that superstition the whole way.

However, I do stick to some routine. I always sit on the sixth seat on the bus, and always next to Tommy Gemmell, but I always run on to the park as the fifth player.

John Clark used to go right ahead of me, now it's Jim Brogan, and Bobby Lennox comes behind me.

Billy McNeill always wanders round the dressing-room with

only his jersey and underpants on until the minute before we get the signal to go on to the park . . . I hope he doesn't forget one day!

And Tommy Gemmell always bangs the ball straight into the back of the net as soon as we get on the field, just watch him the next time.

Why do players believe in it? It's simple, it's all in the imagination, and it's just a way of reassurance. We know the result won't really be changed because of where we sit on the bus, there are a lot more factors than that, but it helps us just the same.

Sometimes, not long before the game, we don't know the team. We have a pool of eighteen players, every one of them is capable of playing in the first team.

I admit it, I feel I should be playing every game. Whenever I am not playing I am disappointed, even although I know it's not possible every match.

I even wanted to play in the international team again. I was upset I was the only one of the 1967 European Cup team who was never capped. I must admit that rankled a bit.

Maybe it is because football is my life. And when you get older in the game you realise how short a career it really is . . . I can remember incidents in games that happened ten years ago as if it were yesterday.

However, before we all start getting misty-eyed together, just let me say that when I lose the desire to go on a football field, and I am quite content to sit in the stand, then I'll know, before anyone needs to tell me, that it will be good-bye Bertie Auld.

Where did he get that hat? But Bertie Auld does not care as he holds aloft in salute to the crowd, a Leeds United jersey after Celtic's European Cup triumph at Hampden

The Young Ones

Another trophy for the Parkhead sideboard, this time it's the
Reserve League Cup which the young ones collected after an
aggregate victory over Dunfermline

THE trophies sit gleaming on the Parkhead sideboard, the
Reserve League Championship and the Reserve League Cup,
as lovingly cared for as any of the top team's honours.

And while the coach parties who, from time to time filter

through Celtic Park on their sight-seeing mission, might occasionally miss their trophies, their significance is not missed by the men who run the club.

This is the investment for the future . . . the assurance that the young ones of Parkhead have the same urgent competitive spirit as any of the glamour names of the first team.

The problem for any club is that no matter how well their League team is doing—the shop window of any outfit—a footballer's career span is relatively short, so they must always look over their shoulder to see who follows on.

For the Celtic side of the late fifties and the early sixties the problem was that so many of their youngsters—the ones labelled the 'Kelly Kids'—were pitchforked into the jungle of First Division football before they were really ready to face all the problems.

I cannot see that happening to the Celtic starlets of the seventies. Some have been tried in the first team, youngsters like right-half Kenny Dalgleish and inside-forward Victor Davidson, and shown glimmers of notable promise.

Some, slightly older, have already established themselves in the first-team pool, like right-back David Hay and George Connelly.

Jock Stein has a dream of keeping Celtic at the top by 'freshening up the team', one of his favourite sayings.

That means simply that he is trying to avoid the traps which Spurs, one of the most skilful sides of the sixties fell into when they let an entire side grow old together.

It means an assurance for the babes of Celtic that if they show talent they will be given the chance to challenge for a first-team place . . . and what youngster could ask for more?

So far, under Stein, the starlets to graduate with the highest honours are Hay and Connelly.

The displays of David Hay with his powerful overlapping against Leeds United in the European Cup semi-final shot him into the very top rank of British players.

These two games won him three international caps in the British international championship. And one leading critic— Brian Glanville of the *Sunday Times*—never particularly pro-Scottish, named him as right-back in a best of Britain side.

Hay is the prototype of the player of the seventies. As easily at home at full-back as he is in midfield, to such an extent that manager Stein still admits: 'We just don't know his best position yet.'

He is the all-purpose player every manager dreams about discovering. Two seasons ago he was centre-half in the reserve side, last season he was in the midfield for Scotland against Wales and England . . . and for Celtic in one memorable Scottish Cup game when he marked Rangers captain John Greig right out of the game.

Still shy in his dealings with the Press, Hay has yet to receive the real adulation which a closer aquaintance with the football publicity machine will ensure. At the moment this youngster—undoubtedly the find of 1969–70—allows his actions on the field to do all the talking for him . . . and he deserves all the praise he has so far collected.

I cannot recall a first-season youngster ever before pushing for the Scottish Football Writers' Association 'Player of the Year' trophy as he did last year, and it could be only a matter of time before he collects the coveted award.

For Connelly, too, a bright football future beckons. The youngster, who first became known to Celtic fans as a 16 year old when he did a juggling act with a football during the interval of a European match, has outgrown that stage . . . the interval entertainment can take care of itself, he is now part of the main show.

The incredible maturity of Connelly was shown in the most testing crucible for any youngster, the 1969 'Old Firm' Scottish Cup Final.

It is the kind of game that can cause experienced players to lose their sleep for a fortnight by the knowledge that any slip-up in defence, any failure to snap a chance will be remembered by fans 10 years after a similar mistake in any other match has been long forgotten.

Young Connelly was listed at outside-right that day to take the place of the suspended Jimmy Johnstone, and his glory moment came when he scored his side's third vital goal just before the interval.

He fastened on to a mix-up between Rangers' 'keeper Norrie Martin and their captain, John Greig, and drifted around the 'keeper to score.

'An old head on young shoulders' was his manager's verdict. But the commentary on the goal itself by Connelly after the game showed all the cool nonchalance which characterises his play on the park.

'I never thought of finishing off the move any other way. When I saw the 'keeper running out to challenge me it seemed the right thing to take the ball past him and place it in the empty goal.'

The style of soccer, 1970. A smoothly-dressed George Connelly leans against his Jaguar to pose for a picture at the end of a day's training

Time off . . . for David Hay as he practises his golf in one of the few spare moments he had in his busy break-through year

And as if he had been describing a goal in a bounce five-a-side match instead of a tension-racked Cup Final, he added: 'I did just what I thought should be done.'

Eventually when the time comes that Billy McNeill will finally call finish to his glorious career, then young Connelly will step in at centre-level.

He has had experience right through to European level—remember his goal against Leeds?—yet the secret with youngsters is not in seeing their ability when they are in their early twenties . . . it's in spotting their potential as 14, 15 or 16 year olds.

And, in fact, for master Connelly at 15 there was fierce competition to Celtic from the manager of Dunfermline at the time, Jock Stein.

He was then only 5 ft. 8 in. tall and weighed in at a mere $9\frac{1}{2}$ stone. Today he is over 6 ft., and 13 stone, see what I mean about spotting potential?

Another youngster, they form an inseparable trio on trips abroad, who staked a claim for a permanent first-team place was Louis Macari.

The busy little man, with the lock of black hair falling over his face, popped up either on the wing or at inside-forward, and the ball usually ended in the opponent's net.

And to prove how he has matured in one season he admitted: 'Two years ago if the boss had told me I would have been playing for the first team I would have been scared to try things. Now. I don't turn a hair.'

He made an extremely valuable contribution in the competition which, more than any other, tests a team's resources . . . the League championship.

The problem for any youngster who steps out of a reserve side into the glare of the First Division is immediately the difference in pace.

Reserve football tends to dull the edges of a player's game, to take away the vital sharpness.

A player with perhaps a middle-of-the-league side can be allowed a few games to adjust himself to the change in environment.

For a player with Celtic there can be no such luxury. Thousands of eyes will be running a soccer X-ray over him, ready to give an instant opinion on whether he will be able to slot into the first team.

Yet I wonder if the supporters do realise what a great gulf there is between First Division football and reserve team soccer.

Like almost every other reporter I get only an odd chance to look in at a reserve match. I saw only three of Celtic's last season.

Two of the games were at Parkhead, and one a mini 'Old Firm' fixture at Ibrox, and it was only in the game against Rangers that the atmosphere one always associates with the first team percolated through.

The other two games were played in front of an audience of only a few hundred, a mere fraction compared to the box office at any First Division match in which Celtic are involved.

So I salute the youngsters for the enthusiasm which they put into their work, and the eagerness they showed for the game.

And it must have been a source of satisfaction to assistant manager Sean Fallon, the man in charge of the reserve side, that his team won their championship with a majority of youngsters in the side.

It is reasonably easy for a club with the resources of Celtic to sweep their way to a reserve championship by packing the team

The shape of things to come . . . a flash-back to 16-year-old George Connelly showing the ball-juggling act which he performed for Celtic fans at a European game

with eight or nine full first-team players. The trophy may look good, but it proves nothing for the future.

Behind the scenes with Sean Fallon there are two of his old team mates, Willie Fernie, the trainer with the reserve team, and chief scout John Higgins, helping in that marvellous ability Celtic seem to have to slot in their ex-players with an eye to continuing the club's great traditions.

Who will make the break-through in the next season? My money would be on Victor Davidson, the inside-forward with the old-fashioned look, even his pants seem a bit baggy by modern standards, and the old-fashioned soccer subtlety.

Of course, players who shine in the reserve team frequently fail in the more testing conditions of the League side.

So far the majority of the graduates from Celtic's soccer academy have been successes when they were given the chance, a tribute to the Parkhead soccer school system.

I know that manager Jock Stein sometimes wishes he was able to give to the kids on his staff the time he managed when he was the club's chief coach to the class of 1957–58, which included such noted names as McNeill and Pat Crerand.

But he still keeps a close eye on the 'young fellas' as he tags them. He will often leave the first team in their training camp at Seamill or Troon to dash up to Glasgow to watch the reserve match.

And surely the ultimate compliment as to how important they are in Celtic's scheme was paid to them last spring when the manager turned down an invitation to a reception by the Prime Minister at Number 10 Downing Street because the reserves had a match that night.

It was near the time when perhaps the worst moment of any manager's year comes around, and a decision must be made as to whether or not any youngsters must be freed.

Jock Stein felt it was more important that he should study his youngsters, and the vital effect it might have on some of their futures, than travel to London.

A football club is like a conveyor belt, no matter how many stars are at the top in the League side there must always be younger talent pushing along behind them.

So the Kelly Kids of the early sixties matured into the European Cup winners, I am certain that today's reserve side at Parkhead will have just as bright a future when their chance comes.